Best of Series C

Interviews with India's Leading Founders and Changemakers at Masters' Union

Best of Series C

Interviews with India's Leading Founders and Changemakers at Masters' Union

Conceptualized by

Published by

A BOUND IMPRINT

Copyright © Pratham Mittal

Published in India in 2025 by Moments.

Pratham Mittal asserts the moral right to be identified as the author of this work.

Printed in India

ISBN: 978-81-970262-6-3

All rights reserved. This book or any portion thereof may not be reproduced or used in any manner whatsoever without the express written permission of the publisher except for the use of brief quotations in a book review.

Contents

Introduction — vii

1. **From McKinsey to Building High-Growth Startups like OYO and Swiggy**
   In conversation with Rohit Kapoor, CEO of Food Marketplace, Swiggy — 1

2. **From ₹600 Cr Deficit to ₹600+ Cr Profit**
   In conversation with Deep Kalra, Founder and Chairman of MakeMyTrip — 15

3. **Beyond Functionality: Power of Personalized Interior Design**
   In conversation with Saurabh Jain, CEO of Livspace — 33

4. **The Reality of FMCG Trends**
   In conversation with Shiv Shivakumar, Former Chairman and CEO of PepsiCo — 47

5. **The Dharma of Business and Filmmaking**
   In conversation with Karan Johar, Executive Chairman of Dharma Productions — 61

6. **The 11 p.m. Calls That Built The Moms Co**
   In conversation with Malika and Mohit Sadani, Founders and CEOs of The Moms Co — 79

7. **The Salesman's Mindset: Building Relationships and Driving Growth**
   In conversation with Kaustubh Kulkarni, Senior Country Officer and Vice Chairman of J.P.Morgan India — 99

8. **How Zepto Delivers in 10 Minutes**
   In conversation with Kaivalya Vohra, Founder of Zepto — **111**

9. **The Many Faces and Emotions of Chai**
   In conversation with Dev Arora, Former CEO of Chai Point — **129**

10. **Gamer to Game Changer: The All-Out Approach to Gaming in India**
    In conversation with Dilsher Malhi, Founderand CEO of Zupee — **141**

11. **The No Broker Approach to Real Estate in India**
    In conversation with Saurabh Garg, Co-founder and CBO of NoBroker — **161**

12. **One Ultimate Failure to One Solid Successful Venture**
    In conversation with Kavin Bharti Mittal, Founder and CEO of Hike — **175**

13. **Lessons from Military and Entrepreneurship**
    In conversation with Richard Pattle, Pilot and Co-Founder of True Beacon — **189**

14. **The Whole Truth and Transparency**
    In conversation with Shashank Mehta, Founder and CEO of The Whole Truth Foods — **203**

15. **Building on Coffee in Unusual Ways**
    In conversation with Tarun Sharma, Co-Founder and CEO of mCaffeine — **215**

Introduction

My journey in education began long before Masters' Union. Coming from a family deeply involved in academia—my father, Ashok, and my mother, Rashmi, serve as the chancellor and pro-chancellor of LPU (Lovely Professional University)—I have always been surrounded by discussions on the future of education. Before founding Masters' Union, I also had experience launching a bootstrapped startup in the U.S., which gave me firsthand insights into the challenges of building and scaling a business.

Masters' Union is not a traditional business school. It was founded with the vision of reimagining business education by ensuring students learn business by doing business. Our programs prioritize practical, real-world problem-solving, allowing students to gain insights directly from CXOs and industry leaders. The Alt-MBA approach we employ moves beyond conventional academics, immersing students in live projects that simulate real entrepreneurial challenges.

This book brings forth the experiences of entrepreneurs from diverse industries—technology, cinema, food and beverage, cosmetics, and beauty—yet they share a common thread: The tenacity to take their ventures to the next level. Their stories highlight the challenges and decisions that shape companies as they scale, offering practical insights into what it takes to achieve this level of growth.

We launched the Series C podcast in 2023 where industry leaders shared their experiences and lessons learned. The insights shared by these accomplished entrepreneurs were too valuable to be confined to just one medium. We wanted to ensure that these lessons reach a wider audience, serving as a guide for aspiring entrepreneurs, business leaders, and students alike. In this book, we have curated some of the best conversations we have had on the podcast to this date.

Swiggy's Rohit Kapoor got into startups after working with giants like McKinsey. Deep Kalra of MakeMyTrip almost went bankrupt during the pandemic, bouncing back with a 600-crore profit. Karan Johar figured out how to balance big, bold films with very real budgets. Shiv Shivakumar shares what it's like to be the longest-serving leader at the second-largest F&B giant. Saurabh Garg started NoBroker simply because he was done paying ridiculous brokerage fees.

Their stories provide invaluable lessons on what it takes to reach this critical stage, offering insights into the trials, challenges, and triumphs that define the entrepreneurial path.

This publication marks the first in a series of books from Masters' Union, aimed at making learning in entrepreneurship, management, and business building more accessible.

We hope this book serves as a useful resource for those navigating the complex landscape of business growth.

Happy reading!

Pratham Mittal
Masters' Union

Rohit Kapoor

Rohit Kapoor has been an accomplished business leader and is the CEO of the food marketplace segment at Swiggy. He has worked across many marquee names, including Oyo, McKinsey, and Max Healthcare. Rohit is an alumnus of ISB and has steered Swiggy through rapid growth, with a relentless focus on transforming the food delivery landscape.

CHAPTER 1

From McKinsey to Building High-Growth Startups like OYO and Swiggy

In conversation with Rohit Kapoor, CEO of Food Marketplace, Swiggy

---

Through his unique strategies and hands-on approach to business, Rohit delves into Swiggy's journey and growth with a narrower focus on his innovative strategies. His unique perspective on transitioning from consulting to corporate roles, and eventually to the startup ecosystem, is no less than a strategic and mindful turn. In this conversation, Rohit draws from his experiences and offers candid insights into the pressures, acquisitions, challenges, and opportunities that come with working in both established corporations and high-growth startups.

❖ ❖ ❖

As a former consultant myself, I'm curious to know your journey. How did you transition from consulting to corporate roles and eventually to startups?

When I was in consulting, people used to typically do two things when they were moved out: They would join as a head of strategy—because most businesses did not trust them enough to put them in charge of P&L (Profit & Loss) statements immediately—or they would join a venture capital firm. And sometimes, the third segment was business analysts going out and doing an MBA from overseas, or from an Indian institute, like I did, so I think things have really changed, in the sense that I have now seen people really stepping out of these boxes.

My answer is of less relevance, and hence it will be interesting to know about what is 'not useful'. Vinod Khosla once tweeted, 'I can't imagine having one life to live and spending it working at McKinsey.' In my opinion, spending two or three years in a place is absolutely fantastic because you develop a toolkit and there are different ways through which you can build those toolkits. You do not need to be in consulting jobs to do that. The question is: Are you focused on developing the toolkit? In a way, consulting forces you to develop one since it involves real-life concepts and situations around some basic concepts like problem-solving, communication, and interpersonal and client management.

In essence, I experienced what it is like to attend college when I was at McKinsey and not when I was actually attending college. It may not make sense, but that is how I felt. Consulting, as a profession, pushes you to grind yourself in such a deep way that you burn out soon. But after that, people choose from multiple options and different paths. Some people have spent thirty years at McKinsey; I spent ten, but I know people who say spending just two years is enough, and now people are going into all kinds of roles.

I've seen tons of people start up. I have invested in at least five to ten McKinsey startups. People join startups, they go to NGOs (non-governmental organizations), and even join venture capital or private equity. It has really become full range now, but it is true that the McKinsey network, even today, is one club I am grateful to be a part of. We have a WhatsApp group of about 700 or 800 ex-McKinsey people, and there are probably around 300 CEOs in that group. Every venture capital founder in India and at least twenty founders whose companies are worth more than $500 million are somehow connected. Now, those are the good things. And about bad things—well, I cannot imagine too many. In hindsight, I felt I spent four years too many.

You spent ten years at McKinsey. What was the trigger to leave? What was the point where you said, 'No, I need to jump into a corporate', and geared toward startups?

The trigger was silly, but I am glad it happened. I was always a fast tracker, and for one review cycle in my life, I did not get to the next level at the speed I had imagined for myself. It was then that I said to myself, 'That's it. I don't want to be here. I will go and do things where I can get more speed.' It was extremely silly, almost myopic on my part, to think like that. But in that environment, I did think that way. That was my trigger, to be honest. I can cook up another story, but that will not be a true one. I was simply not on the fastest track, according to my own silly internal benchmarks, something I completely discourage you from following. I think this is not good for anyone's mental health. But I am glad it happened because I was so comfortable there, and I was coasting. I would have never done what I ended up doing if that hadn't happened. I truly felt bad at that point in time, but it turned out to be the best trigger I ever got in my life.

And then, why startups?

I had joined Max Healthcare, which was not exactly a startup even back then. When I had joined it, Max Group was already thirty years old, and in 2017, I was co-leading Max Healthcare. This segment of business was to be sold to KKR (Kohlberg Kravis Roberts & Co. Inc.) at that point, and I said that my job was done, as I had come in with a certain objective of making it valuable. The value analysis had happened, and there was a genuine buyer. The promoters were mostly excited, and simultaneously, I was thinking of my next stint. Of course they suggested I should stay in the group and do different things.

What are called mature industries today were seen as revolutionary around six years ago. So don't believe anything you hear too much. Uber and Ola were becoming a part of my life, and I was also using Zomato, Swiggy, and tons of other applications. That was the time it struck me that something was happening in the startup ecosystem, and with my age, I felt I didn't have a window to wait much longer. I analyzed it and said to myself, 'Let's explore and figure out if I can do something.' I was very scared about it because the stories that came out about senior people joining startups weren't always pretty. I did not know the culture well enough. I asked around and made a short list of the companies that were able to integrate senior folks well. I say senior only because of my age, not my competence...there is no entitlement here, and trust me on this: Two of them were OYO and Swiggy. So Swiggy was on my list even back then.

Consultants get used to being uncomfortable pushing their limits, and startups can be challenging because there is a lot of action going on. How would you say the challenges were different in the startup ecosystem compared to the corporates?

The pressure is everywhere, so there is no point in ranking it by saying this pressure is smaller or this context is harder. These things were different and depended on anecdotes. So what I did was, I spoke to a bunch of people who are already in the startup sector, and I asked them, 'What does it take to succeed?'

> *The one difference I have found in the two ecosystems, at least in the places I have worked, is that if I focused on performance, I did not have to bother too much about anything else.*

Ananya Tripathi, the former CEO of WhiteHat Jr. was one person I knew, since I was her manager at McKinsey. I called her and asked, 'Ananya, you've been working in the startup ecosystem for a while, so what do you think?' Being a straight talker, she said, 'There is a lot of noise, so don't focus too much on it. Just focus on your performance—everything else will take care of itself. Because otherwise you will get a lot of bad advice.' And that just struck me in the right place.

The one difference I have found in the two ecosystems, at least in the places I have worked, is that if I focused on performance, I did not have to bother too much about anything else. In many companies, the culture is such that one doesn't get to know who is who, and there is less pressure. Startups are architected in a way that there is first growth and profitability to be pursued. And it is fast-paced, so if you are performing well and using your talent optimally, then you are likely to get a little further ahead than you would in a more established setup because the hierarchies are not very well established in a startup. So it is easier for a young person who is really good to get responsibilities way ahead of tenure. Because one cares about the performance, not the tenure, in the broader scenario. That is the first difference.

Second, the technology orientation is very different. My exposure to technology till I left Max Healthcare was that I used mobile phones, laptops, and MS Excel and Word. But that changed dramatically. I now understand how to scale using technology as compared to scaling only through people or processes. That is genuinely something you cannot imagine and understand till you are a part of a setup that thinks about that first. For example, when you think of distribution, we will not say, let's hire a thousand people's workforce. Instead, we will first think about the highest velocity distribution possible through a digital mechanism. And then, if it needs people, it needs people. That's the bottom line, and those are some of the differences you can witness. But the places I'm leading or working at are not small anymore, so I am sure there are other versions of startups that are far more agile.

At one point, you mentioned that you don't want to become an incumbent soon, which means that you need to continue to drive innovation to your model. At that scale, how do you see the thought process towards innovation change compared to when companies are much smaller and there's a large canvas to paint on?

In my opinion, what keeps companies ahead is not necessarily innovation, though it is the most talked-about thing. On the contrary, what actually keeps companies continuously ahead is outstanding execution, which is very underrated. When I say we don't want to become an incumbent, the ideal situation is that anybody looking at the machine operating from an execution standpoint should be able to say that it is difficult to fight them. That, combined with innovation, is a really big moat. For example, you order and receive food—that's under my domain. That model is what Food Marketplace is—which I lead—and is also the largest segment of our business. That requires innovation plus immense execution. And it's probably one of the most complicated businesses I have run because of the very simple fact that different stakeholders need to be satisfied within thirty minutes, millions of times, every single day. But some businesses are pre-PMF (Product-Market Fit), and their execution has less relevance. Ideation, finding the customer truth, thinking of PMF, and thinking about how to scale altogether is a problem in the beginning. So, think small, and then grow with it and move on to the next level.

Now, at that scale, you are also thinking of adding verticals. For example, Swiggy Instamart. How do leaders go about thinking when to build versus when to buy?

To start with, we have a significant builder mindset as a company. The analytical way to think about it is to look at share capital and understand what percentage will be diluted for acquisition. Swiggy's equity capital has been diluted in fewer numbers for acquisition compared to other large startups. We love to play with clay, as they say, and mould things.

There have been cases where we have bought or found an immediate fit or an outstanding team. For example, Dineout is a business we want, and I run it in addition to the food delivery model since these are complementary to each other. The founders have the right vision, and they have scaled the company the right way. What we will create will not be any superior to what they have already built, so it's much easier to get them into a fold if it is possible, and then we scale it up. But other than that, more or less we have a builder mindset.

Would you say that depends on the company?

Truth be told, acquisitions are incredibly hard. The most overused and under-delivered word in business is 'synergy'. If we bring in as much synergy as we talk about, things will drastically change for the better. In terms of acquisition, sometimes these are very valuable. Look at Instagram or WhatsApp: Without these, Meta would have looked very different today.

> *Acquisitions are incredibly hard. The most overused and under-delivered word in business is 'synergy'. If we bring in as much synergy as we talk about, things will drastically change for the better.*

One challenge is operational scale; the other is when you are at scale and making sure you continue to be a team of A players, and evidently, maintaining talent and culture. How do you ensure that?

It is almost axiomatic to say A-players are the most valuable. I think the focus should be put on both A- and B-players, and the job I have is to not have C-players. Having the right mix of players is crucial, as A-players can be expensive, so you also need B-players who have the potential and drive to become A-players. As long as attitude and values are in the right place, then the job of leaders gets easier.

What are your thoughts on being a CEO when you are not a founder? There is a lot of debate about whether founders should step back and let someone else run the show when companies scale up.

My wife is a founder of a small business, but I don't want to be one. So, there is absolutely no right answer. However, one thing is clear: If you're the CEO or a founder, the founder has to warn the CEO. Nobody would have succeeded without Larry Page's and Sergey Brin's sponsorship. They have the maturity and the wisdom to let people prosper. The fact lies in understanding what the founder is really good at and if the joy of what they want to do is to take the company to where it needs to go. The problem arises when founders believe their work is complete, only to painfully realize later that it isn't. However, sometimes they struggle with or fail to enjoy the 'learning' part of the process. For example, for a company, building on compliances may be very important if they are in a regulated sector, like FinTech. But if the founder does not enjoy being in meetings with legal departments and compliance teams and understanding RBI issues, then it gets tricky.

If you are in that situation, get somebody who can do that and enjoys running things differently. I think being at peace is crucial. If I am the CEO, and there's something I'm responsible for, where I know the founder is much better than me, then I will pull them in, day in and day out, and let them control it.

What is your take on management graduates?

My take is quite mixed. The first issue is that what you are doing while being in the institute is not what you are expected to do after graduating. The gap between the two is large. Sometimes, there are a lot of choices, which bring in some entitlement with it. I love people who forget where they came from, what degrees they hold and instead are absolutely passionate about the job at hand. My grandfather used to say that even if you have to clean the floors, tell yourself that no one can clean the floors better than you. As long as I find people with that spirit, then I care less about whether they are MBA graduates or undergraduates or no graduates at all. That passion and grit are missing sometimes. People are thinking too far ahead in the future all the time, and it's a disservice they do to themselves. On day one, they're already thinking about a day two years later.

People ask, 'What is my career path?' It's the most stupid question to ask. Nobody knows the answer to that. If you push too much, you'll get a bullshit answer. The correct questions to ask are: What do you identify as talent in the company? What creates your best people exhibit? Who's your most successful salesperson in this company, and what does she do differently?

Any individual who shows up at work with a certain level of compensation has to be good at two out of the four things and outstanding in at least one. It could be either of the four: Problem solving, communication, understanding P&L and numbers or understanding people. Look at the case study method: It is so archaic; it existed and had value in a place when there was no internet, a time when somebody had to go out and research, put four pages together for you to understand what exactly happened. But today, why is that method even needed? People should research on their own, talk to people, Google things, interact with ChatGPT, and come back with an educated answer. I think management education has to go back to basics and say, fix these four things. People don't know basic concepts like VLOOKUP, and these people are from tier-1 MBA colleges.

Additionally, there are certain subjects which are quite important and useful. Like manual accounting to understand the concepts of 'build versus buy'. Management education should be only four things: One, is to fix the four aforementioned ideas; second, expose the people to different people and situations so that they have perspective, and third, think independently and critically. Do not get swayed by what you last read on Twitter. I have no problems with Twitter or any social media platform; I am heavily active on it, but I don't form my viewpoints based on just anything I read on those platforms. Fourth, there are certain management concepts (like 'build versus buy' or CAPM [Capital Asset Pricing Model]) which are so pervasive that they should be known. All these aspects combined forms a good foundation for management education, and eventually that person who understands it becomes valuable.

Is consulting a safe bet post-MBA, or should one directly jump into startups?

It is as safe as anything else, so you should do it. Consulting works very well in some scenarios; so, in today's world, if you are not too sure where to head, then consulting is a great position to be in. I am saying it is a great option because it exposes you to options and choices, and you end up working on ten projects in three years. Plus, one gets the finishing degree, so you won't go wrong. The great human network one builds through consulting is absolutely priceless, and the whole network becomes a helpline for relevant events.

What should be the key focus in the initial strategy for launching a business similar to Swiggy or OYO, where the dependency lies on the delivery partners, riders or hotels?

Think of them like a consumer. What will you do if you are to offer something to a consumer? What is it they want to do but cannot achieve in today's construct? It could be acquiring more customers, or it could involve digital distribution—something they might not fully understand or know how to implement. It could be any problem statement, as long as the problem statement is clear. Consumerization, consumer type thinking, for any cohort, is a valuable asset. At Swiggy, we think like that about our delivery partners also because we have a three-sided marketplace, not just a two-sided one. And then rolling back and saying, find your first 100 loved partners who will love you. Don't focus on economics so badly that you don't even experiment with what could work and what could not work. Pushing early startups to absolute profitability very early on is not necessarily the brightest idea because it reduces the scope for experimentation and innovation. In today's world, think about what is the scale-up through technology and digital segment that you can do.

What are your thoughts on startups that copy ideas from the West?

I don't want to be original for the sake of being original. Now, Apple is not always first to market, but it is the largest cash flow generating machine on this planet. This is because they come with a much superior product, at least in my eyes, and there is so much love to generate for their products. Besides, the nature of where the economies are today allows for category experimentations to be at a much wider canvas. For example, pet food. A large number of households in the U.S. have pets, and the market is so wide that you can carry out many experiments with a variety of foods. For India, it will take some time to get there. There is no problem in accepting the fact that we are heading in that direction. Now, people talk of China, but China created a walled garden. They went in a regulatory regime which is very, very different. So, while you have innovation, you have new things, you also have certain ways of living and society which you will not be comfortable with. We, as a society, are quite entrepreneurial and innovative.

Capital availability is a recent phenomenon. Anything that happened in the last ten years, for me, is recent because countries develop through thirty-, forty-year cycles. Now, at this point, one may think that this is copying. For me, it's mostly evolution.

What would you change as a student if you were back in your MBA days, and what are your top two learnings?

First, I would have developed more relationships. I knew everyone… all of the 349 students. I know them by name, but I wish I had better relationships with them because that's something we still have as a currency. Second, what you should do is take your chances and don't blindly fall for advice that can create contradictions in your mind. Back then, I wanted to be the president of the student body, and someone told me that if you do this, your grades would go down. I think I would have scored exactly what I did and could have been the president of the student body if I had stood for the selections. Introspect a little and take time to think about what life you want, what the pathways are, and look at people five to ten years down the line. How have they reached destinations that you want in your career? And then try and focus on those things, rather than doing everything that you get served.

Deep Kalra

Deep Kalra has pioneered online travel in India. Since starting MakeMyTrip in 2000, he has brought brands like Goibibo and redBus into the fold and turned the MakeMyTrip group into a leading online travel company and the largest e-commerce business in India.

Beyond travel, he plays a pivotal role in shaping India's digital economy. As a founding member of IndiaTech.Org, he supports homegrown internet companies.

CHAPTER 2

From ₹600 Cr Deficit to ₹600+ Cr Profit

In conversation with Deep Kalra, Founder and Chairman of MakeMyTrip

---

In this conversation, Deep reflects on the immense challenges the travel industry faced during the COVID-19 pandemic and the tough decisions they took to navigate MakeMyTrip through the crisis. He shares his vision for sustainable tourism—one that prioritizes proper infrastructure, accessible amenities, and unforgettable, repeatable experiences.

As a leader, Deep discusses the art of balancing data-driven decisions with intuition, the importance of staying closely connected to customers, and why fostering a culture of innovation and experimentation is key to long-term success.

◆◆◆

What are your thoughts on the country's education system and how it has evolved? How does this change compare to what you observe at Masters' Union today?

Truth be told, Masters' Union has all the founding blocks in place, and with the kind of vision the founding team has, it will put India on the map. Speaking of role models, Masters' Union once hosted one of my biggest role models—Sanjeev Bikhchandani, for the convocation event. He has been my role model since I started working.

In this day and age, there's no dearth of demand but quality supply has always been a bane in education. Sadly, that's India's story. When we meet foreigners, they love to tell you, 'Oh my God, you speak such good English.' And now my response typically is, 'Yours is not too bad either.' Because, realistically, most of them were colonized the same way we were. But more seriously, they ask, 'Why do Indians do so well overseas and everywhere else?' To set some context, there are probably ten Indian CEOs on the Fortune 100 list and maybe twenty on the Fortune 200 list. The reason for that is that our education system is so rigorous, that we have beaten up metal and beaten up gold to make it ready for anything, but it's not there at scale. Masters' Union is looking to change that. There is something very special about being around in the early days of an organization. One feels a sense of connection and a significant part of the process. When I look back at my undergraduate days, I wish I had invested more time and mindspace into it, and I would have gotten more out of it. The more you put in, the more you'll get out of it. Clearly, Masters' Union is a place that wants to give more and it's up to you how much you churn out of it—that's the same for business education.

What do you think is missing in the Indian education system that prevents us from retaining Indian students or attracting international talent? Despite advancements like 5G and a massive internet user base of 120 crore, higher education still accounts for 10% of the country's trade deficit. What needs to change?

Firstly, it's scale and quality: There are not enough high-quality institutes in the country. It's a pyramid: At the top, there are the world's best institutes, and then there is a deep chasm. They fall off because those were set up with investments often made by the government. Ashoka University is a new and unique model which is arguably the largest group philanthropy project in India. Similarly, FLAME University, Symbiosis International University, and Manipal Academy are doing a good job but these are very few and far between. One has to count beyond the IITs and the IIMs. Delhi University, which boasts of fantastic colleges, has stagnated now. As someone who graduated from St. Stephen's—and my wife from Lady Shri Ram College—I've seen firsthand how much potential Delhi University had. However, the curriculum hasn't paced well. I graduated in 1990, and the changes made since are just a few, while the businesses and economics in general have all changed dramatically. So if you're not nimble and alive with the time, then it could be a downhill slope.

Secondly, there is affordability. So 'trickle down' theory has worked: A lot of household incomes have quadrupled. I use my example as a reference point because when I graduated school, only five or six who belonged to rich business families made their way overseas, the rest found their place in India. Today, more than 50% of a batch from great schools are going overseas to study. It's sad because they're not getting good colleges to attend over here. Eventually, it boils down to the question of why youngsters, despite their affordability conscience, go abroad to colleges that are as good as colleges in India. We need Masters' Union to be on steroids. The beauty about something different and something unique being done, Masters' Union being one great example, is fantastic because India is very entrepreneurial.

As someone leading an empire generating over half a billion dollars in annual revenue, what does a typical day or week look like for you? How has your routine evolved over the years, especially in the post-COVID era?

I had the unenviable job of reporting a 96% drop in revenues; we were obliterated because of the nationwide lockdown. In a weird sort of way, that was a good thing that had happened, just like the other shocks that had happened in the past. The truth is, the better companies not only survive, they figure out a way to thrive. The tough moments push you to the corner and force you to make very tough decisions.

> *Tough times mean tough decisions. But it also means better companies will survive and weaker companies will sadly disappear. I've seen that happen now in four or five cycles.*

We had to cut costs, but it couldn't happen overnight. We took a lot of pride in never having to do layoffs but six months into COVID, we had to let go of 10% of our workforce. In the twenty-three years of MakeMyTrip's history, it was not the worst decision, but I would say it was certainly the toughest and the most distasteful one.

We took many silent vows at that and tried to help everyone personally and get them jobs. There were also some ex-employees we tried to bring back, but it was a very tough task. From a similar standpoint, it makes you address all the other frivolous costs (even that has a cascading effect). Therefore, an asset-light model is super smart. If one observes the pre-COVID situation and the present post-COVID times, we moved from minus ₹600 crore to plus ₹600 crore. A sharp swing of ₹1200 crore happened in this two-and-a-half, three-year period; and that was the game changer. It would not have happened if we weren't pushed to the corner. The market did question its sustainability. However, during the last quarter, we got the full reward, and the stock now is much closer to where it should be.

Like all entrepreneurs, I believe it can be better, but it took a while and, in a way, validated the tough decisions we took. Tough times mean tough decisions but it also means better companies will survive and the weaker companies will sadly disappear. I've seen that happen now in four or five cycles. Back in 2001, when 9/11 happened, it changed the world of travel. People didn't want to get onto a plane for several months, and our business was entirely U.S. and India-based. Then, the SARS (Severe Acute Respiratory Syndrome) epidemic happened, and during the same time the dot com bust had happened, so no one wanted to fund a company like ours. It was these terrible times that made us tough. The toughest thing to do in a very difficult time is to carry on and that's the lesson I learned. After that, no crisis seemed that crazy or that existentialist in nature.

During such times, only two things work. One is your left brain, which focuses your attention on metrics and numbers. You have to go down to the very core concepts: Cost of customer acquisition and repeat rate. In Masters' Union's case, once you get an employer on board for recruitment, why should they ever go away? They would only go away if they didn't like the people they hired from here, but if you've done a good job it's okay to incentivize your first-time trial.

The tougher thing is the right side of the brain, which is really fuzzy logic, or what I call thinking from the gut. There's a very good book called *The Clever Guts Diet*. 25% of the neurons that we have in our brain are there in our gut. One quarter of your brain is in your gut. Some of you are very brainy and thus your gut is also very brainy. Thinking from the gut actually is an instinct reaction. For business leaders, it can be invaluable but cannot be a daily strategy. And that's where discipline comes in—so we developed what I call discipline and depression. Every month we took stock and I told my two senior guys that if we commit to something, we commit for a whole month. No second-guessing, because from a team of twenty-four, including us, the twenty-one people are watching us closely. Our second-guessing could make them feel uncertain about their jobs, eventually leading them to find jobs for themselves, and very rightly so. So we ensured we stayed in, not out. If you lead with discipline and instinct, you can do wonders.

The third thing, that was driving me, was a fear of failure, a term I realized much later for myself. I had done an entrepreneurial stint in the past, and I had tried very hard for four years to make it work but that was a failure. I knew that if I failed again, two dots would make a line, and I wouldn't have the courage to try another venture. So the fear of failure had crept in. It also stems from some amount of self-esteem. Ego is a bad word, but self-esteem is not, and there's a fine line. Ego is a terrible thing to have in business. One needs to have no ego at all because business is the most important thing. One has got to swallow their pride, talk to partners, and extend the olive branch because they have to do what's right for the business. But self-esteem is very important since it will drive you harder and harder to say, 'Let's not do the easiest thing in a tough time,' which is shut shop because you'll never have the guts to come back again. The toughest thing to do is say, 'Let's eat this out a little longer.'

You've spoken about some of the silent vows you took when you had to make tough decisions. Are there any of those vows you would like to share?

Apart from my silent vows, there are some core values as well. There's a direct correlation between the culture of a company and the founders' values, in my opinion. From a certain point of view, it's a manifestation of the founders' values, but a good organization should be very open to being moulded. Every time you have a new senior hire, you should be quite open to saying, 'Let the goodness that this new person is bringing into the company be absorbed. Let's be very open and not rigid.' We are very open to someone bringing a good idea or a new way of working. It could be from anywhere that person has worked. Usually, it comes from very young people, but then you've got to be the kind of organization that says, 'Why don't we look at this?' One shouldn't be scared to come up with great ideas and the day we become a company where people are afraid to speak their minds; it is the beginning of the end.

I have been embarrassed at many board meetings by my colleagues, and it's very tough initially because you're meant to be the founder. But if there's merit in it, it's a good thing. It's equally great if you can develop a way of saying, 'Okay, let's evaluate that.' But again, it comes down to not having an ego because the moment you have it, you think how can someone else have a better idea than me? Sometimes, great ideas emerge in the moment. Ideally, they should be discussed before the board meeting, but you have to allow for spontaneity. Perhaps something sparked it off at the board meeting itself.

> *One shouldn't be scared to come up with great ideas but the day MakeMyTrip becomes a company where people are afraid to speak their mind; it is the beginning of the end.*

Back in the day, our board meetings would go on for not just an hour but a whole day; and often someone would have a great idea at an off-site, completely away from work setups. It's reasonable to think that something could have gotten sparked off by that. And that's why that individual in your senior team spoke up at that one point in time. The message that the action of speaking up sends to the rest of the organization is that it's worth its weight in gold, because the next person says, 'Oh, wow, it's perfectly okay to say what I feel, which doesn't happen in most companies.' We ask people to not bother too much about couching, or fancy presentations because if we lose the power of the idea coming from a youngster who is much closer to our customer than we ever will be, we get further and further away.

I love doing customer labs because they are very insightful. I observe about eight or nine in-depth interviews, led by a professional moderator. I like to meet someone who buys flights from us, not hotels; then meet someone who buys hotels from us in the next week, but not homestays; someone who buys homestays from Airbnb, but not from us. Designing these cohorts and gaining insights is invaluable. The second reason I do it is because if I go, others go, and others take it seriously. The beginning of the end is when you feel 'I know my customer.' Today in India, it is impossible to know your customer, irrespective of what you do. If, right now, I were to guess which kind of school you have come from, where you belong to, which city you've come from, socio-economic profile, I think I would fail. And I play this game with myself all the time when I'm on a flight. The customer is very different today, and I am amazed to know who is filling up our hotels and our flights. It boils down to the same thing: Trickle-down theory. $2,000 per capita income is racing to $6,000 but they're not the people buying from us. People who are buying from us are in tier-3 towns, who have so much money that they don't know what to do with it. They just need the opportunity. There are people who come down to Delhi for the weekend regularly, stay at five-star properties and just shop. Many high-end malls are alive today because of the largest tier-2 and tier-3 towns, not tier tier-1 towns because people from tier-1 towns are going overseas.

And luckily for us, youngsters have declared and decided that they'll travel. It is right on top of their list—and that was not the case when we were growing up. We'd go on a family trip up to the hills, once a year, followed by a trip to our grandparents' houses, as a customary thing in India. Later, as I got married, we went overseas—it was unheard of, we counted our pennies but did take that trip. And suddenly, now people are going for as many as eight times a year. I play a game where I ask how many trips you made last year. There was one girl, who along with her husband had travelled each weekend of the year—double income and no kids—but that's how it was. And often these are people who are joining us at starting salaries. The choice of travelling is more about taking a break than about the concern of money. Many of them are not saving money for a car, or investing in a house so these choices are easier to come by.

How do you balance maximizing profits while prioritizing environmental sustainability? How do you ensure that smaller towns aren't over-travelled and face the negative impacts of over-tourism?

It's definitely not easy. One can have the liberty of doing these things when you scale up and mature as a company. We didn't think much about CSR (Corporate social responsibility) in the early days, but we certainly gave time to NGOs (non-government organizations) who are as old as us as a company. Udayan Care, for example. In the early days, every Sunday, many of us would go and spend two hours teaching the kids there, most of whom are orphans. We've hired girls from there as well, and it's an amazing partnership.

I always say there's only one negative of travel: Carbon footprint. Unless you are the Forrest Gump of India, that's how it has been. India's ecosystem is very fragile and over-tourism has denuded most of our hills. The disasters that have happened in Himachal Pradesh and Uttarakhand are very sad reminders of this. Deforestation has eroded soil cover and on top of it, we've allowed people to build shops, houses, and restaurants right next to the rivers. These disasters lead to people losing lives; and these scenarios are mirrored in Manali, Shimla, Nainital, and other such towns. We cannot let it happen to other places.

Many people who book through MakeMyTrip consciously give a small token to MMT Foundation, which works with many organizations. We have planted close to 2 million saplings through our association with Seva Mandir. In Andamans, we have tried to rid one entire island, Neil Island, which is smaller than Havelock, of single-use plastic. Additionally, we built three water ATMs and got Tata Chemicals to anchor them, as the groundwater there is pretty clean. We give reusable bottles to all our travellers, and one can get water for one rupee from a water ATM, which is run by an Adivasi woman. The government has reciprocated by banning plastic bottles with less than one-litre capacity. The goal is to make the entire archipelago of Andaman and Nicobar free of single-use plastic. It's incredible to think that there are now whole islands of plastic floating in the ocean. We've taken it upon ourselves to look at sustainable travel as the only future.

Goa and Shimla have both been significantly impacted by over-tourism. From a policy perspective and within the travel industry, how do you see this challenge being addressed proactively rather than reactively?

While some state governments recognize the potential of tourism, the industry continues to struggle with perception—it is neither a preferred career choice for professionals nor a priority sector for top IAS (Indian Administrative Service) officers or ministers. It's a sad reality. The Centre can't impact states, so we're working with both the state and Centre. Apart from Rajasthan, Madhya Pradesh, and Kerala, not many states get tourism. What those in leadership positions need to ask is: Why will people keep coming back here? They will come back for the experience, not just to see a monument again, but for the entire end-to-end experience—road conditions, accessibility, decent infrastructure of public restrooms, and so on. Eventually, they will see what they have come to see, but whether their whole experience was interesting depends on the state, the town, or the city it is in. I really wish I could change things at that level.

Many obvious and easy ideas have already disappeared, but what are some of your favourite ideas that still hold potential? How should students go about ideating and developing such concepts?

Since I was there in the early days of the internet in India, the idea of online travel was a no-brainer. I learned about businesses that were being done on the phone, and I figured they would move online. My two plans were online stock broking and online travel, both of which moved online very quickly. In a way, it was an easier time, but in many other ways, it was tough. Raising $2 million in funding then was tougher than getting $50 or $100 million today. An equally big challenge was to convince high-quality people to give up their jobs and come to work for something like this. The very thought of it was crazy.

> *If one has a bent for tech, can think logically, and break down problems into small pieces then they can build businesses on AI itself.*

Now, AI has opened up a new realm of possibilities. It is as big as two other things were in the past: Computers in the early '90s, and then mobiles and smartphones with computing powers. I am confident that AI is going to change the game in ways none of us can fathom. So if one has a bent for tech, can think logically, and break down problems into small pieces then they can build businesses on AI itself.

One can build many businesses because they are experiencing them today. Many of those who are from tier-2 and tier-3 towns can see the gap in the market and eventually create offline businesses that work well in those domains, which others won't understand. One has to play to their strengths, play to something which they are innately good at. One's chances of success will go up 10x. But every time they try to get into something that they are not good at, then A: They are going to labour through it, and B: They are not going to enjoy it, eventually bringing their chances of success down by 90%.

It took me three years to realize banking is not for me. People who love banking are doing very well, but I wasn't loving banking. The most important thing to do is to figure out what makes you tick, and think about this long and hard. What makes you tick, what is it you get excited about when you are alone and have a lot of time? That thing will be very close and in tandem with what you're good at. Figure out what you're good at—marketing, finance, stats, numbers, math—it could be anything and if you're better than most people, you're by default in the top 10%, and then just work on that. These are the days of super specialization. Gone are the days of being a generalist.

Once you find what you are extremely good at and specialize in it, success will be much easier for you. Specialization could be in anything—for example, listening to people and understanding their troubles. Maybe you'll build something around the whole counselling side of the business which is becoming huge. Mental health in India has largely been ignored till now. But if you fall into the trap of going where the most money is, you might just keep struggling and you'll never go ahead than those to whom it came naturally.

What made you list on Nasdaq in 2010? If MakeMyTrip were to list today, would Dalal Street be the way to go?

It came as a surprise to all of us, because it was the January board meeting of 2010, and our board was split in the middle, with Sanjeev

Bikhchandani on the board too. Sanjeev looked at our numbers and said in a flash, 'You guys are ready to list.' Then it was a question of U.S. versus India. In India, Info Edge was the only listed dot com and, in the U.S., there were at least fifty listed dot coms, including many from overseas. At that point, we still had at least 15% of our business coming from India. Our numbers were good—$400 million top line, revenues going to about $60 million, growing at about 50%.

The international investors were keen on us. We had Tiger Global with visitor rights, Saif Partners, who was our first investor, and we had Sierra and Helion. We were all quite confused and the discussions were not going anywhere. So I said, 'Give me a week.'

In such situations, I go back to my first principle—if I don't know something, I admit it openly. I took that week to talk to ten people who had experience in listings. I remember reaching out to Nandan Nilekani, whom I know now, but he was a stranger back then. Soon I was put in touch with Mohandas Pai, another one of my classmates from Ahmedabad, Chandan Prasad, and others whose opinions were very insightful. After these conversations, it was clear that a U.S. listing would be better because of the model's understanding, the appreciation of the model, and the depth of the market. Eventually, if you do well, you get rewarded very well. You do badly, you get it back harshly. But the Indian market, in the past four or five years, has definitely opened up to internet stocks. So a dual listing is something we are open to considering. It is hard, but there is a big value in being listed in your home market.

Your belief is to fail often and fail fast so you can learn. How did you balance the instincts of failure and success within you and how has your attitude changed over the years?

It's a fine line. There is an overarching fear of total failure, and then there are small things, like features, products, and experiments. The core aspect is that one needs to build a culture where it's okay to fail. When I attend product meetings and if people have taken the right steps, then I support them. That's what sponsorship is all about—where one person offers you sponsorship and believes a particular idea is worth pursuing. You have to take a leap of faith, and you also have to build a culture where people are comfortable coming up and saying, I want to build something crazy.

Moreover, the secret sauce to competing—many would assume it to be discounting the prices further down—but the actual secret sauce would be one thing that can't be replicated. Even for Amazon, which you can say is the cheapest place, their secret sauce is not discounts or cheap pricing. Their secret sauce is under the hood—it could be backend sourcing, the assortment, the logic, the recommendation engine, and so on. The bottom line is that one has to think very hard about what their secret sauce is. In fact, people who have tried four or five different things get rewarded in different ways because they are the many entrepreneurs one really wants; and if you are the one who likes experimenting, then you must join companies that allow you to experiment. This is not something very pervasive in bigger conglomerates but surely there are some others which one can join.

MakeMyTrip advertisements have evolved over the years. What convinced you to have Alia Bhatt and Ranveer Singh as the faces of MakeMyTrip? What impact did it have on your customers and what was their overall reaction?

It was actually MakeMyTrip who had paired them together for the first time, which Ranveer fondly remembered at the premier of *Gully Boy* when I met him. We got very lucky with them. It took a long time for me to get on board and I was actually convinced by my CMO. His point was that we are now going beyond just air tickets and we need to drill into people's minds that we do hotel bookings, and a powerful voice can be very helpful in establishing that. We did rigorous research to look at many pairs, and many individuals, and eventually took a leap of faith; it was our gut instinct and belief in our CMO back then. Funnily enough, I love it when someone says, 'Trust me, this will work' because it takes some conviction to say that. But since I am the most gullible person, I *will* trust you, and later I'll come get your throat if it doesn't work. It's true that they are putting their reputation on it and saying, 'I will make this work'.

However, the risk with a celebrity is: What if that celebrity does something that goes against our brand ethos? And that's why many individuals were rejected. But there's only so much one can do, to judge someone's character.

Many companies like Microsoft have AI-powered engines now, that will soon integrate pins with a feature that will help consumers by sharing the best booking options available. How would you factor in the person's choice, be it of hotels or other travel requirements?

About eight years ago, we invested in a company called Inspirock, before AI was even a thing. Inspirock was a travel planner built by two brilliant IITians, and I was blown away by what this engine could do. They had built an engine wherein you just had to give commands of where you want to go, how many days, what your budget is, and they'd build a complete itinerary for you. Inspirock later got bought by Klarna, which was another platform whose model was book now, pay later.

> *The future is smart AI recommendation: No one is going to spend too much time on planning, which is otherwise a very complicated thing, rather they are going to spend that time enjoying the trip.*

AI is now doing all of that and challenging that. We are excitedly building something around the question that was asked. We have a very close partnership with Microsoft but we want to build some core IP (Intellectual Property) for travel, which remains with us. That is the future: No one is going to spend too much time on planning, which is otherwise a very complicated thing, rather they are going to spend that time enjoying the trip. By just giving the basic parameters, you're going to get great and selective options customized for you, despite the same inputs. Recommendations, and at that, smart AI-generated recommendations are the future. For a consumer who has given a platform like ours all their preferences around meals, seats, age, departure time preference—getting a smart recommendation is a very sincere expectation to have.

Saurabh Jain

Saurabh Jain, co-founder and CEO of Livspace, which attained unicorn status in 2022, has handled multiple operational responsibilities at the Home Interior Design and Renovation Service company. Having worked across geographies and industries in the past, Saurabh, a qualified textile engineer with his dynamic leadership, continues to steer Livspace from strength to strength.

The IIT & ISB alumnus is a key player in the home interior design market and is responsible for building strategies and acquiring a solid customer base at Livspace.

CHAPTER 3

Beyond Functionality: Power of Personalized Interior Design

In conversation with Saurabh Jain, CEO of Livspace

Saurabh Jain, CEO of Livspace, outlines the shifting dynamics of the real estate sector and how it impacted the interior design industry during the COVID pandemic. From the pandemic's immediate impact on construction to the booming demand for design services once restrictions eased up, the conversation touches on the unique trajectory of the industry.

The conversation takes the reader through Saurabh's personal journey behind the company's growth, shedding light on the decision-making process, early acquisitions, and the entrepreneurial mindset that drives Livspace. Reflecting on lessons learned, from fundraising to building a strong team culture, he shares the company's approach to leadership, stress management, and the importance of adaptability in an ever-changing market.

❖❖❖

How is the business doing, and what is being brewed at Livspace?

The entire business ecosystem has gone through a sharp transition post-COVID, and each segment has seen its unique trajectory of recovery and growth. The interior design industry is a derivative of real estate and has witnessed both impact and growth. During the COVID lockdown, constructions were stopped with an immediate effect, and that resulted in limited inventory. The construction lag, coupled with limited inventory and sustained demand, led to the prices going up. The pandemic also caused property buyers to postpone their decisions to buy and rent properties since there was extreme uncertainty around them. In this dynamic scenario, where the demand was sustained and even went higher after a point, with supply being limited, the market was reshaped.

However, after the pandemic days were over, the surge in demand caused our business to witness a boom since it is an extension of the real estate industry. We are yet to unfold the entire impact it had on a national level, but so far, the fundamentals of buying houses have been accelerating our services and offering new opportunities for us, making it a good time for us to be in this business.

Buying versus renting: Which is more practical?

Buying a house has never been a very mathematical decision, rather an emotional one. More often than not, an individual doesn't drive that decision but their family and the lifestyle they are focusing on does. Like the many purchases we make, even house buying cannot be rational or mathematical. In fact, we make money because the decision is not mathematical. If it was, then this business is like a commodity, and we won't make money—there's no delta. The more emotional and complex the decision is, higher the chances are of business generating margins.

This is a service-based business with a deeply emotional consumer base. Given the many opportunities in product-based automation, do you ever regret choosing this path?

After nearly nine years of running this business, one factor that we critically focus on is personalization at scale. As a core concept, the interior designing business or service is fundamentally unscalable due to the customization the customer asks for and the bespoke nature of it. Since the value chain doesn't have any economies of scale, the industry should remain fragmented and small.

However, in the business ecosystem, now there are technology, innovation, and business structures that, if leveraged correctly, can effectively serve any kind of consumer. Personalization at scale means that one still gets the chosen service or product at affordable rates without compromising on quality. Personalization is a very nascent concept in India, with only a few industries trying to do it today, so there is a massive opportunity to scale. Be it jewellery, the home sector, interiors, fashion, or even cars—consumers need a touch of customization.

The question we need to answer is: Are our value chains agile enough that we can balance scalability with customization and transform our ideas significantly towards bespoke services and products?

> *After nearly nine years of running this business, one factor that we critically focus on is personalization at scale. As a core concept, interior designing business or service is fundamentally unscalable due to the customization the customer asks for and the bespoke nature of it.*

How does that work in a real-life scenario? Is there a template created beforehand for categories that help in personalization?

In today's world, when a builder constructs a standard 3-BHK as a bare shell, the largest items that one requires for their homes are wardrobes, TV units, storage, etc. Fundamentally, those are built by using 70% wood, and in the modular arrangements, there are panels, which, when joined, make a whole unit. Understanding and delving into the setup further, you go to the bottom of the economics of those panels with their various sizes, widths, depths, etc. When you instill technology in it by showing 3D setups on a screen, the customer gets the choice to change the dimensions and drag and drop items. So when you merge technology with the bulk buying of raw materials with agile manufacturing, you can build a solid 70% to 80% of a template for consumers. Templatize it to the core, from bottom up—from the raw material to intermediate product to finished product, and that gives customers a million choices which helps you scale personalization.

When you're trying to scale personalization, does the NPS (Net Promoter Scope) invariably go down?

Initially, yes, owing to the solutions that are half-baked, which are hard to digest for the consumers of those solutions. While forming any solution, a lot of manual intervention is required to stitch the imperfect solutions for making a perfect one. During that stage, the NPS tends to be moderate, but being an organized player, as you gain scale in a fragmented sector, you tend to move the market along with you, which drastically changes the NPS.

The reason being, to everybody around you, you are such a big account that has premium technology and processes in place, and that contributes to the fact that you can dictate quite a lot. It's then that the inflection point of NPS comes in. There is scale in personalized problems, but only if you are able to achieve that, you'll see a new life; else, death comes easier in between the zero to moderate levels.

What did your journey look like, and how did the company change over time?

When we started, we were just a bunch of passionate people, unaware of the industry or its dynamics. The focus was soon directed on how consumers feel about the need for a solution. If we take ourselves as consumers moving to a new city, how would we get the interior designing done since we don't know any individual contractors around, and trusting a new one with ₹10 or ₹15 lakh isn't easy. That's not the kind of purchase that our generation or target consumer makes. The way to go about it is to identify the problem statement and chase that. Go back to the root problem and start bottom up. Consider what consumers need depending on their persona.

Right when you started, was the intention to build a platform or create a service that solves a problem?

The realization that we have to build it like a platform had hit early on. If we were to build it like a service-only model, then we'd be like any other larger design studio, something we didn't want to pursue. We wanted to componentize and put a platform model to a lot of things; how that would happen was a separate thought process and journey. We tried to devise it after many conversations with potential consumers. We desired to be in their shoes to trickle down further to create a solution that caters to their needs. It took a couple of years to bring it into shape.

What was your first fundraiser story like?

It was very different for me than many other founders. I started a company named DezignUp after graduating from the Indian School of Business (ISB) and tried my hand at consulting at Accenture. By then, Livspace was already operational in Bengaluru, and we, at DezignUp were trying to do something similar to what Livspace did, but naturally, they were doing it more extensively than us. Less than a year into DezignUp, it got acquired by Livspace, which was founded by Anuj Srivastava and Ramakant Sharma, and that's when I joined hands with them.

What was your thought process like when you built a company from scratch and decided to exit or merge within just a year? What factors influenced that decision?

The Internet was growing rapidly back in 2014–15, and services from

Internet-first companies were at a nascent stage. DezignUp began with an idea to help those who are not sure where to buy things from or get services done in their homes. The momentum in the market was towards a certain direction, and fortunately, that wave worked for us when we merged with Livspace. In a way, we predicted that trend and went ahead with it. Startups of those times evolved in phases, and those very startups focused on services instead of products.

Since the fundraising began after DezignUp was merged with Livspace, was it straightforward to raise funds since you were following the trend, or was it difficult to get through?

Fundraising is never easy, regardless of the market situation. In the first round, we raised about $4 to $5 million, and while approaching VCs, we had our thesis in place. That thesis constituted the persona, customer segment, size of the market of those moving houses, and potentially how much we can capture. To reach the proof points, however, we had to go through a lot, and that comes only when you go along.

How many customers did you have before you raised your first round, and do you believe the number would be sufficient if you were to raise the same amount today?

At our monthly run rate, we had about eight to ten customers, but since our model is complex, that is a good starting point. Whether a particular number is enough varies for each industry. Additionally, it's quite important to have clarity—what are you building, what kind of scaling is required, and what customers are going to take for you to take it higher.

How long did you work at Accenture, and do you feel that time was enough? Looking back, would you have preferred to start your own company right away, or did your experience at Accenture play a crucial role in shaping your entrepreneurial journey?

I pursued consulting as a career for three years, and that broadened my horizons of industries and businesses around me. At the time, the company I was consulting for wasn't very established, and we were trying to have our offices in Dubai. Since the beginning, I have had a knack for entrepreneurial roles and wanted to work in uncharted territories that come with no templates of their own. Even during the times I would work on these roles, I did taste a bit of success and feedback that motivated me to pursue those roles further. That leap of faith in my case was a very big one since I had the liability to pay back the education loan I had taken. But if certain processes and templates work for a particular person, then you must try those out.

Was pursuing an MBA helpful?

It was, but the idea is to get formally introduced to the concepts of businesses that have worked and the frameworks that exist. From the perspective of having awareness, pursuing an MBA has been helpful as after that you'd not repeat the same mistakes that you might have read about or people around you have made. All of this helps people discover themselves. While I was studying at ISB, I discovered my interest areas, zones which are difficult for me to deal with, if I will be required to hire people who are great at things I am not, among other things.

What segments do you hire people for, and what do you prefer doing yourself?

My focus areas are interacting with consumers and staying deeply involved in the new product development processes. Two qualities I certainly look for in those I hire are their passion and smartness. They should be very entrepreneurial and have the same vision that I have. 99% of my work as an operating leader revolves around finding the right people for the job since they would be the ones I will spend most of my time with. I often go back to the principles we had inculcated within ourselves during our college days, principles that make teams and groups work together despite their disagreements on a certain thing. I look for such qualities while hiring.

> *I often go back to the principles we had inculcated within ourselves during the college days, principles that make teams and groups work together despite their disagreements on a certain thing.*

How can one check for that in an interview?

Checking for analytical skills is easy since there are many frameworks and tests available these days. The real observation lies in intellectual honesty and truth. As an employer, one must be able to share what they are building and looking for, and more often than not, they will be hearing the truth from the other end. That's where the equations actually start. I tend to be very clear about what we are building, what the challenges are, fuzzy roles, etc., and that lets the interviewee decide what their motive should be for joining us.

Owing to the ongoing debates around work-life balance, do you believe that one must work for seventy hours a week?

For a creator, founder, or founding team member, creation stems from excessive passion. When you are this passionate, you often don't see the clock. Back when we were building our concepts, working round the clock didn't take a mental toll on us, even if situations were tricky. It's true for any artist or a functional leader. We were enjoying what we were trying to build and still enjoy that.

> *For a creator, founder, or founding team member, creation stems from excessive passion.*

What does your day look like?

I am a meticulous planner, and my calendar is my navigating tool. So my weekly, bi-weekly and sometimes even monthly meetings are organized perfectly well in my calendar to avoid chaos. Further, I'd colour code them to ensure I don't miss the ones where my complete attention is required. Everyone has limited energy, so my focus is to push the important tasks and meetings up. My work starts at 6 a.m. and by 8 a.m. I would have delegated tasks and responded to those who needed my inputs. After that, my mental bandwidth is free, so I can focus on other tasks. That tends to be over-planned because I am the sole actor in that. A good 30% of our days would go in brainstorming sessions around new products, launches, etc., and the remaining 70% stays around the ongoing work, review meetings, and ensuring nothing goes off track.

Another focus of mine is on connecting with team members beyond the meetings. Be it over lunch, coffee, or meeting after office hours, because I tend to get stressed wondering if I am really connected with people and the system.

In a traditional setup, 10% of the workforce carries a lot more weight than the remaining 90%. What is that 10% doing differently from the remaining 90% that really helps them stand out in their teams?

One must have an entrepreneurial bent of mind—which extends to one person owning a segment of the work. Back during the days of COVID, we had aimed to increase the number of cities we are functional in from four to forty. The ongoing questions were how to expand, how to hire, and how to open a retail centre, among others. It was a bold claim, but we managed to open in many tier-2 cities during that year to an extent that each week there was one centre across the country.

It further encouraged us to make playbooks of the retail centres, and the documentation was so crisp that anyone could seek help from it, read it, and understand the process. The second is to stay humble and honest to the core, regardless of your role, position, or experience. If one is unaware of something, they need to admit it and seek help.

Third is to be a great team player, as that can change the dynamics of a good team. As many processes are multi-functional and cross-functional, being a great team player helps a team achieve the end point of a roadmap.

How can one know if they are a good team player?

A good team player embraces collaboration over individual glory. They come with a clear vision and roadmap for themselves and for others to achieve heights. Even if that requires someone to adjust, get rid of rigidness, and over-communicate in some scenarios, they do it head-on and achieve it. Ownership of leading a team comes to the one who has visualized it. Otherwise, eventually, it can become a burden.

How do you manage the stress that comes with bad reviews?

Customer review essentially is feedback, so that certainly leads to stress. The kind of business we are in, the customer tends to be emotional and because it's about their home, we can't go wrong. Our focus is primarily on how to right the wrong and help the customer who has been affected. We then share this within our system so no one else experiences it the next time. We learn and try to ensure that it doesn't happen again, but it's a never-ending work of learning and trying to improve.

What is the first thing you do when you come across such stressful times?

I try to dedicate my next few days very intensively to that. Instead of taking weeks to correct that, we try to channel our energy so that we can probably achieve 70% to 80% of it and get it over with.

The United States and other countries have many big companies that are building great content around houses and professionals.

They charge the consumers based on the discovery model. Have you tried a similar one in India?

DezignUp started with that model, but what we realized at Livspace was that an Indian consumer values underwritten promises a lot. Many purchases are not made on the open market, and it's a fact that customers need a lot of trust. That is something we are trying to solve: The trust deficit. The geographies that have bigger companies have probably evolved beyond the trust deficit, and maybe in those geographies, unlike in India, the government interventions are foolproof, and agreements are in better shape.

At your level, how important is it to micromanage the company's functions as compared to just taking strategic decisions?

When a company is established, everything involves micromanaging because it is still being built from scratch. Typical business fundamentals don't work or get applied when you are just beginning. At that point, you would want to get the work done, whether through micromanagement or macro-management. Now, micromanagement is definitely not required if you have the right team alongside.

How has Livspace been affected by consumers' increased knowledge around sustainability? How have your practices changed to make your products more sustainable, and where do you see yourself in the future regarding sustainability?

This topic is more critical for the organized players who are in the overall construction and home improvement business. Livspace, an organized player for interiors, is already making plywood and using chemicals that are much better than the unorganized players, considering the sustainability factor. Furthermore, consumer education and government intervention are two critical factors to bring more sustainable practices into play. Many countries are already deep into following sustainable practices, and within five years, hopefully, we'll be there too.

Shiv Shivakumar

PEPSICO

Shiv Shivakumar is a former Chairperson and CEO of PepsiCo India Holdings Private Limited and continues to be one of India's longest-serving CEOs. Being a management thinker and a leader who aims for absolute focus, Shiv's career has been marked by strong leadership, wherein he has contributed to making informed decisions and strategic directions.

Shiv plays a pivotal advisory role, serving on the Board of Governors for IIM Udaipur, XLRI, Xavier University, Great Lakes, and SPJIMR business schools. His contributions drive the integration of innovative management practices in these institutions.

CHAPTER 4

The Reality of FMCG Trends

In conversation with Shiv Shivakumar,
Former Chairman and CEO of PepsiCo

In this conversation, Shiv Shivakumar takes a closer look at the current state of the CPG (Consumer Packaged Goods) industry, the dramatic shifts in consumer behaviour, and how the digital landscape has evolved and transformed the consumer's choices. He also discusses how the industry's traditional approach to distribution, brand management, and innovation is being challenged by tech-driven startups and agile new brands.

Beyond the obvious, he delves further into highlighting the importance of cultural understanding and local partnerships when managing multinational teams and markets. And how, while starting a career, one must focus on building deep expertise and navigating the waters at full throttle.

❖❖❖

You have a vast array of experience in the consumer goods and technology space. Before diving deeper into the CPG industry, could you describe what your professional journey looked like, and how did you pick this field?

In life, one never knows what they are good at. It's surprising but true. In my case, however, I'd say there were some defining moments. When I was in boarding school many moons ago, we were asked to write an essay on the radio. My first line said, 'I'm asked to write about an invention from Marconi Blatch.' There was a teacher, Mrs Mark, who used to teach us English and had a profound influence on many of us. When the time came for her to distribute the marksheets, I got the most—a solid sixty-six on hundred. This number seems very low compared to the marks of today, but during those days, the marks didn't flow like water; they were hard to get by. After giving the sheets, she said, 'Shiv, you write well; don't ever give up this habit.' No one tells that to a ten-year-old—neither parents, uncles and aunts, nor anyone else. For a teacher to say that was huge and that stuck with me, so I've consistently written throughout my life. I was an editor during my school and college days and have written regularly for the business press.

When I was at IIT, I was deeply involved in co-curricular activities and served as the students' secretary. A few of my seniors—Shanti Kumar, Sanath Rajan, T.M. Narayanan, and Anand Reddy—saw potential in me and encouraged me to pursue management. It was during my second year in college, back in the '80s, that they tapped into a potential even I could not. It was then that I was fascinated by the idea of marketing and dived deeper into its theoretical concepts. It was true that we were applying those principles, unknowingly, during our college and school days, but it was at IIM that I truly gained a full-circle understanding of what we had been practicing all along.

A topic of fun and banter was that I was so eager to learn that I wrote to the top professors across the world during my days at IIM—from Peter Drucker and Ted Levitt to Benson Shapiro. I said, 'I like this article of yours. Can you send me more?' And I would get about twenty to thirty articles that would make a huge stack. So, a joke that formed was how I was already professorial and not inclined to do an MBA.

Eventually, I realized that if I am to pursue marketing, then I must sharpen my skills. I worked hard and landed in the right places. My advice would be to understand that others are a better judge of you and your strengths than you are. Fundamentally, there are two types of people: Over-the-top, arrogant, and boastful, or reasonable, but others see in you that you cannot see in yourself. I come from a family of bureaucrats and doctors, so for me to not be one was a very different journey and a disappointing one for my parents in the beginning.

What are some of the key trends that are shaping the CPG industry today, and what are the changes in consumer behaviour that are driving those shifts in the industry?

By definition, the CPG or FMCG (Fast-Moving Consumer Goods) industry consists of daily-use products that are stocked in multiple outlets. Historically, consumer product companies did not have any control over the distribution channel. In the whole chain, the wholesaler controlled which stock to keep and which would be sold to retailers. Procter & Gamble, P&G as they are commonly known, was one of the first companies in the FMCG market. They went to the wholesaler, who controlled the market at that point, and requested, 'Can we put a poster near your shop?' Not knowing what the future held, the wholesaler agreed. The poster said, 'Ivory, the soap that floats,' and this was one of the very early days of innovation and advertising. Suddenly, the retailers would come and ask for that very soap. That's how branding started, and branding as a marketing trick only started with posters in the FMCG industry.

Soon, the bigger companies realized they could control distribution and started approaching retailers and serving them as long as they had economically viable quantities. When television started, P&G was the first company in India to sponsor TV serials, and they were a soap company, so the term 'soap opera' came into being. In the 1900s, FMCG saw the biggest innovation: The barcode. Barcodes were first used by Wrigley, and what a barcode did was make it seamless for everyone to check inventory and price. FMCG also uniquely pioneered the concept of management: Brand management as one knows it today.

The concept of brand management was started in P&G on 13 May 1931, when Neil McElroy wrote the famous note on brand men. Then came along category management, which was started by Colgate Global. All these companies were at the forefront of early packaging innovation, early distribution innovation, and early management innovation, and that's why they had their standing in the market.

In India, however, FMCG companies have always controlled distribution and believed that the more distributed you are, the better it is. In a completely digital world, this is not a strength anymore. Secondly, the FMCG companies thought they owned the brand and knew how to do brand marketing. Thirdly, which was unique to India, all of them ran on negative working capital, which means that what they paid their supplier system was more than the money they got from their distributors. These were the three fundamental concerns.

In comparison, if one looks at the industry today, distribution is no longer a strength. A small brand can run and get past the bigger ones. Earlier, it used to take years to build a brand; now, it's easier with the digital advantage. In my opinion, FMCG companies have become very slow. In today's world, who are the agile ones? The answer is tech companies. FMCG companies have consistently lost their agility in embracing technology. For example, these companies did not partner with organized trade in India and did not partner with Facebook, Google, or Amazon, where the future lies. These companies have much more data about their consumers and price points than the FMCG companies would ever have on their consumers. FMCG is at a crossroads. If they do not effectively partner with technology ecosystems, then their days are numbered.

This could explain the rise of D2C (direct-to-consumer) brands like Mamaearth and Bombay Shaving Company. While these companies are gaining traction, legacy giants who once dominated similar categories, like HUL (Hindustan Unilever Limited) and P&G, are now choosing to invest in D2C startups rather than

launching their tech-driven brands that cater to both online and offline markets.

In FMCG, the strategy is to identify a need and launch a variant. However, sometimes, these very companies go overboard. I used to run haircare for Unilever, and at one point in time, P&G, our competitor, had seventy-two variants of shampoo. It's crazy—there's no need for seventy-two variants when ideally, there aren't seventy-two types of hair. Each brand manager would introduce a new variant, and eventually, nothing would stick. The problem is that the sales teams gets overwhelmed and don't know how to sell all these variants, making what seemed like a great idea in the boardroom fall flat in the market. Take sulfate-free shampoo as an example, it has always been there in the market. But for a big company to put it out and even sell one ton would be a Herculean task because they are not used to small volume, whereas small companies think big volume. That's one fundamental difference. Big companies have committees. Small companies have commitments. Big companies have proven records, while smaller ones have a hunger to say that they want to beat the big guy. Regardless of which sized company you are in, one must think like a small company person because that's how you'll succeed.

The degree to which a small company can target their audience, even virtually, is massive, and that very degree of sharpshooting has actually helped a lot of small companies do far better. Even if the bigger companies had tapped into the potential of what small companies are launching, they were simply unwilling to execute it. The top IIMs have existed for over seventy years, and not much has changed. As a board member who encourages them to change, I can tell that not much has changed. What does that tell you? That tells me there's an inertia, and often in big organizations, in big teams there's an inertia and arrogance that stops them; nothing else. The day one becomes humble and says, I want to learn and try and play small experiments and that I'd rather try it and fail rather than judge its destiny without even trying.

> *The degree to which a small company can target their audience, even virtually, is massive, and that very degree of sharpshooting has actually helped a lot of small companies do far better.*

PepsiCo is a leading brand and continues to be a market leader for a while now. Considering how smaller companies are taking over through their iterations and experiments, how did you drive innovation at PepsiCo?

Regardless of the kind of business you lead, it's critical to anticipate how the same brand will generate revenue half a decade or a decade later. It certainly will not be the same way it's generated today. Take B-Schools for example; currently, their dominant source of income is fees; a decade later, I can assure you it will not be the case. Sure, it will be one model, but not the dominant one.

Secondly, analyse what kind of capabilities and people you require in the future. Bollywood movies are a prime example. Back in the '90s, the success of a movie was all about distribution—how many reels you printed and how many theatres you could get into, and during those days, the ticket prices were capped at six or seven rupees. Suddenly, the government realized that ticket prices are no longer a challenge, and now you have tickets at 200 bucks or 300 bucks. Back in those days, if you ran a movie for two weeks, you were a hit. Now, you have to run it for twenty-five weeks to make it a hit. The focus has shifted from distribution to marketing, with tactics like creating controversy or buzz to fill theatres. The metrics have changed.

Another example from the same segment is how music rights are sold globally today, and you attract a wider audience when the movie gets released. Coupled with your marketing tactics and a wider audience for the first two weeks, the revenue generated is enough, and it's a new capability in itself. So, an industry that actually changed and then didn't change after that is a great example. One has to constantly challenge themselves as an individual and ask what are my skill sets.

Will the same skill sets be valid five years from now? Will the industry I am in be valid five years from now? If you don't ask those questions to yourself, you're going to fall back, whether it's a country, whether it's a company, whether it's an individual, all three will fall back.

Having worked in global MNCs (multinational corporations), you've experienced firsthand how challenging international expansion can be. With cultural differences and varying market needs, companies often struggle to adapt. From your experience, how do companies navigate the complexities of managing global operations and expanding into new markets?

I wrote an article on a similar topic: 'Are multinationals relevant in a future world, and why are they losing?' I looked at the top 100 multinationals. The global GDP (Gross Domestic Product) grew at 3.4% in 2010–2021, and the top 100 multinationals grew at 3.8%. The EdTech companies, however, in the top 100 had grown at about 8.4%. This brings me to the idea that fundamentally, global corporations—whether they are FMCG or not—become giant bureaucracies. The reason is that all information is available to you in the next minute, and the entire decision-making process goes up the chain quickly. One wants the big countries such as ours to only execute, which is a shame, considering that we have people with great brains. Hence, where are multinationals losing? They're losing to small, nimble competitors in each country because they are agile and able to see the opportunity much more. The way to deal with this is to consistently paint the picture with consumer evidence.

Every time we had a visit from overseas, I would ask my team to first take them to the marketplace, visit retailers, observe how products are displayed, and analyze the competition. After that, make them visit consumer homes to understand how they live and buy and where their priorities lie. Then comes the time for a meeting. In many global organizations, when there are such visitors, an argument erupts between the visitor and the nationals on the way they see life. In my opinion, once they observe trade and the consumer, they know better what works in a particular demographic. Mutually, both parties want to grow the brand, so the focus should be on that; differences must be thrown aside. That's how you manage global corporations. This will not change until you truly have an empowered leadership and people are willing to listen more than they're willing to talk in global corporations.

> *The battle is not between brands but between ecosystems. When partnering within an ecosystem, suspend your ego. Focus on growing the pie instead of focusing on which is the bigger or smaller brand.*

Beyond managing the global offices, you were managing stakeholders, along with employees and customers. What are some tips and tricks of sustaining a global corporation and managing it all at once?

The battle is not between brands but between ecosystems, be it managing a global corporation or in India. Take the iOS or Android ecosystem. Those with an Apple iPhone belong to the former ecosystem; those with a Nokia phone belong to the latter. When I entered FMCG, I didn't really worry or think about ecosystems, but during my days at Nokia, I recognized that mobile phones can't be sold if the operator is not successful. One will be surprised to hear that from 2007–10 we tracked the BSNL subscriber base because BSNL used to go rural, and they had better towers than Airtel, Vodafone, or Idea. When Manoj Kohli, CEO of Airtel, suggested launching 1,000 vans to sell mobility in rural India, we teamed up and split the costs fifty-fifty—an initiative that was proven hugely successful.

Later, when I joined Nokia in 2005, India had just 80 million subscribers; today, it's over a billion. We then tapped into the market and recognized that it was women and mothers in rural India who didn't have a mobile phone. Upon asking them why they didn't have one, they reasoned that it cost about ₹1,500, and they didn't need it as their sons and daughters already had one. We juggled a bit and offered a deal to those women that pay ₹75 a week, and after twenty-five weeks, the phone will be yours. They agreed, and we went on our journey to discover this path-breaking model with a microfinance company that would give loans to these women on the condition that it is income-generating. We set the deal, went to Orissa for the pilot with loans and mobile phones in hand, and not a single woman was ready to go ahead with it. The reason was that there was no SIM card. We realized what a mistake we had committed by not thinking of a SIM card, which we assumed the women would go out and buy. Then we circled back to Manoj, who offered SIM cards free of cost as they would then be making money off the SIM cards that would be used by these women. That year, we sold about 2 million phones to women alone. In such cases, our learning was that we needed a microfinance company, a phone, and a SIM card to make it all work, and these three components were critical to our journey. Women would use those loans to set up their retail shops or buy buffalos who would generate enough to pay ₹75 for the phone. We had to show the entire ecosystem and partner with the ecosystem to make it work.

When partnering within an ecosystem, suspend your ego. Focus on growing the pie instead of putting your focus on which is the bigger brand and which is the smaller one. As long as you're expanding the market together and your focus is on the consumer, that makes the whole ecosystem grow.

Amazon is another good example. If they were to sell their own products from day one, they would have failed. Today, more than 50% of the products sold on Amazon are not their own products, and that's the only way to grow the pie.

Could you shed some light on where the CPG industry is headed and where can new startups or new technologies help in the industry?

Some industries that are as obvious as daylight, healthcare and education, are at the forefront. The former comes with a lot of regulations and needs trust from the consumers to operate. The latter needs a solid outcome and guaranteed results to operate. For example, why would somebody send their kids to a school? The outcome there is top ranks.

The third place one can look at in terms of where opportunity could be is the value chain of each industry. If the value chain has inefficiency, then it's a great way to disrupt it. Take distribution as an example. Every industry where the middleman has added no value has been killed. Look at the music industry or a travel agency. We don't see music shops anywhere because the industry has gone completely digital; similarly for travel agents—if they haven't travelled to a particular city, how will they recommend one? In both industries, the middleman added no value, and thus, that segment has died. Think hard about where the middleman has too much money with him and is adding no value to their industry.

Having said that, the biggest problem doctors face in India is an over-informed Indian consumer. They come with their opinions sought from the web and then go to other doctors for a second opinion—none of this happens elsewhere. One needs to use their idea very carefully and ask what is possible. There are many opportunities that are possible as long as you have imagination. I had a fantastic finance professor at Wharton, John Percival, who said something that still rings in my ears. He said, 'Spend imagination before you spend money.' It's so true. For each of these businesses, ask yourself, 'Can I reimagine this business? What part can I do and what part can I build as an ecosystem and partner with?'

Imagination is not a skill that is taught or learned in schools, but being on the board of many B-Schools, what innovation or change do you think is needed so these skills can be taught?

Here's something that will not make me popular, but I'll still mention it. If you're studying 100 case studies, drop half of them. They're not useful. The case study method, which originated from Harvard professors, was the LCAG (Learned, Christensen, Andrews, and Guth) approach, named after the four professors who brought it forth, and then it became the SWOT (Strengths, Weaknesses, Opportunities, and Threats) analysis. While it's a great shorthand for analyzing opportunities and threats, it has its limitations. While doing it, you are a God because you are not involved in the actual decisions. Instead, get people from the industry with real insights and the problems they are facing. Take an example like how Jio is offering IPL (Indian Premier League) viewing for free on Jio Cinema, while Hotstar and Disney have paid x amount of dollars to beam it to your TVs. Such discussions and debates builds critical thinking and helps with hypothesis-building, which are critical to consider in such a fast-changing world.

A case study is a rear-view mirror in which you are looking back, whereas the focus should be on forward-thinking skills. The good thing about the hypothesis is that there's no right or wrong answer, but it's testing your ability to think so the future in all business schools belongs to people who can think structurally, critically, and can imagine a different world. An example to understand hypothesis building is the innovation that IPL brought: Impact players. Imagine if an impact player came to a test match. On day one, you have a pace bowler. Day three, the pitch is spinning, so you bring in a spinner. How interestingly competitive will life be! Test matches will no longer be boring.

> *A case study is a rear-view mirror in which you are looking back, whereas the focus should be on forward-thinking skills.*

Having written a couple of books on the topic, what is your advice to the younger generation who are graduating soon on how they should be thinking of career transitions and the choices they make about their careers?

First, your skill set must be good. Whatever your areas of interest might be—accounting, digital marketing—you should be great at it. Ask yourself what can make you the best in the world—not in a particular city or a graduating batch—and ask yourself what stops you. It's nothing but the effort; the material is already out there for you to conquer.

Secondly, wherever you join, give it at least three years. The relationship is mutual in terms of you taking time in judging the company and them in turn judging you; you have something to learn and so do they. While you are at it, keep learning something new and keep progressing. Money is not the only variable to judge your success. If you have money, it doesn't mean you're good. However, if you're good, money will follow you.

Thirdly, contribute liberally to the ecosystem, especially your alma mater. By doing that, you build not only your personal brand but also your credibility. The best way to know a subject is by actually trying and teaching it. In doing all this, if I were to encapsulate, you need focus. The most successful people are very sharp about what distractions to avoid, however attractive the distractions are. The more distractions you can eliminate, the more successful you will be on the path that you have chosen.

Another example of distraction is when colleges and schools, even the top-tier ones, have twenty to thirty clubs. Being a part of the strategic review committee at a premium B-School, I tell them that there is no point in having so many clubs. No employer judges an applicant's leadership skills based on whether they led a particular club. My advice is always to cut those many clubs to five. Be ruthless and do a great job at those five.

Those five clubs should be co-curricular, not extracurricular clubs. Go with a marketing club, a finance club, an investment club, or a consulting club, and keep them as co-curriculars. Any more than that renders the whole idea useless and leads to distractions that many suggest to avoid.

Karan Johar

A cinema buff at heart and a true Bollywood businessman, Karan Johar has been at the helm of Dharma Productions since 2004. He is an Indian filmmaker, producer, and director, and is the son of acclaimed Hindi film producer Yash Johar.

KJo, as he is commonly known in the industry, made his directorial debut in 1998 with his blockbuster film, Kuch Kuch Hota Hai and has continued to launch great talent and films under the umbrellas of Dharma Productions and its digital content company Dharmatic Entertainment.

CHAPTER 5

The Dharma of Business and Filmmaking

In conversation with Karan Johar,
Executive Chairman of Dharma Productions

In this conversation, Karan Johar takes the reader through his anecdotes on rising in Bollywood, introducing new talent, and the future of Bollywood and Tollywood. Being the face of Dharma Productions, Karan Johar talks about his evaluation of risks while launching and directing movies, his relationship with his colleagues, the stakes at which sensitive decisions are taken, and how to break into the industry as an amateur.

Apart from heading Dharma Productions, Karan Johar is also the host of the sensational TV show *Koffee With Karan* in which he talks about the trends the Indian cinema is witnessing while giving a sneak peak inside the lives of Indian actors and artists.

❖❖❖

What has been your journey like, as an entrepreneur? What did the initial days look like?

There is an interesting blend of humour, drama, and facts attached to that question. Quintessentially, I'm not a business person at heart—numbers evade me. I'm not solid with financial calculations and manipulations, but Apoorva Mehta, who happens to be my childhood friend and the CEO of Dharma Productions, is a finance head and great at those things. It all came crashing down when, back in 2004, my father passed away due to cancer, and I felt all alone. It was my father alone who would manage the business and at that point, I was even clueless about where our funds were.

Imagine the extent of the disconnect—one day after I came back from attending the IIFA (The International Indian Film Academy Awards) awards, my father wanted me to sign some cheques, and I blindly wrote lots of love on them because I was only used to signing autographs back then.

Circling back, one day after my dad's prayer meeting, I was sitting in my office, and a man walked in claiming to be our chartered accountant. He then mentioned that a dear family friend wanted to meet me. That person came with a letter that my dad had left behind for me which had all business matters, none of which were emotional because he knew he had a short life after the diagnosis. He had explained how the business must be carried on, where our investments lay, and whom to trust and not trust. It truly became a Bible for me at that point. The family friend who had brought it, said to me, 'Karan, this is only because he knew you were clueless. And he was so worried and scared while he was alive. Because you wouldn't have wanted this conversation to happen, since it was too emotional at that time.'

So I took that Bible which enlisted bank account details, property investments, etc. and I reached out to Apoorva, who then agreed to leave behind his entire life in London and move back to India overnight. This letter became a reference point for him as well.

> ***Shah Rukh Khan insisted that I make* Kaal, *which is a smaller film, make mistakes with it and learn from them.***

That's how we began: The Dharma Productions that you see in its glory today, actually began like that. Back then, we were making a film called *Kaal*, and I had my doubts about it. Shah Rukh Khan called me and emphasized that I should make it since it's a smaller film. He insisted that I make the film, make mistakes with it, and learn from them. We went on to produce *Kaal*, clueless about the production process or how to sell the film, but we learned that after producing films one after the other. Dharma Productions, as a business model and the studio that we had set up, is quite nascent. It started in 2008 when we produced *Wake Up Sid*, *Dostana*, *I Hate Luv Stories*, and *Kurbaan*, among other films. It all started with two people, Apoorva and I, who were very passionate and were best friends from school and college. The model almost felt like a startup, because we were two people learning on the job, making our mistakes and what kept it going was that we had a deep commitment to the company and a lot of passion to take it forward.

It has been twenty years since you took over Dharma Productions. How has the company evolved? Is it a corporate or does it still feel like a family business at the heart of it?

It's truly a bit of both, but much more inclined to be a family business because I function like that. At Dharma, we have an open-door policy which means I don't need emails if there is an urgent situation—one can simply walk in and get it sorted. Apoorva Mehta, the CEO, is the only one running it like a corporate setup. We'd walk into the office in our track pants like the creatives we are, but he has truly aligned the company to what it is today. If I see him wearing denim trousers, I'd know it's Friday since the company observes Casual Fridays. He is someone who has gotten everything down to the T: The HR department, the POSH department, the legal department, and the financials. We are organized, structured, and disciplined like a corporate.

What is your relationship like with Apoorva? Are there disagreements and fights?

Apoorva and I share a dynamic that balances my creativity with his business acumen. Being a filmmaker, there's a lot of abandon in one's decisions and they are often driven by instincts—which are typically difficult to quantify and explain to someone who has a business-oriented mindset. For example, when Ayan Mukerji walked in and I decided to back him up with production, he was a first-time filmmaker with no significant experience, and people questioned my judgement. I simply mentioned that he is a genius. Now, he has made *Brahmastra*, one of the most expensive films in Bollywood. So even though I could not quantify why I believed in him, I knew I had to.

> *Being a filmmaker, there's a lot of abandon in one's decisions and they are often driven by instincts—which are typically difficult to quantify and explain to someone who has a business-oriented mindset.*

There are also times when I empathize with other filmmakers and directors, being one myself, especially when they share how they are struggling with budgets and are going overboard by a few crores. I tend to give in and then Apoorva steps in. He'll talk about investments, verticals, recoveries, budgets, and P&L (Profit & Loss) costs making sure we don't lose sight of the essential financial markups.

If one wants to be safe on a film, then the recovery from digital rights, satellite rights, music rights, and perceived theatrical earnings should equal the cost of production plus publicity. For example, a movie I am producing has a cost of production of about ₹75 crore, then ₹15 crore for P&L, which makes the total ₹90 crore. If I get ₹40 crore back from digital, ₹20 crore from satellite, and ₹15 crore from music, then I am already at ₹75 crore while my cost was ₹90 crore. With a presumption that my film will do about ₹40 crore, then 55% of that comes home, theatrically, which tells me that I can make this movie. But in these cases, your mind should be able to do these intelligent calculations. However, if you have to take a chance, you will take a chance.

It's like each movie is a startup you're investing in, so you have to do the cash flow analysis.

It's essential because there's a lot of rotation money. Money comes from one place and goes into the other.

For a good two decades, it's clear that a lot of risks were taken, new faces and genres were launched, some bets would have worked, some wouldn't have. Can you share some of the lows you faced that people might not have heard about?

Some movies do excellently when looked at from an outsider's perspective, but not necessarily from a financial point of view. When I was making *Student of the Year*, the film did really well, it did ₹70+ crore with newcomers in it, but I had spent a lot and we were down on that film by about ₹15 to ₹20 crore. I assured Apoorva that we were going to make this up because the lead actors were great and we had signed them for a three-film contract. Soon, we made *Hasee Toh Phasee*, *Two States*, *Badrinath Ki Dulhania*, and *Humpty Sharma Ki Dulhania* all of which had either of the leads from *Student Of The Year*. And these actors were paid a subsidized fee because that was our contract. So eventually that shortfall got covered because of the packaged deal we had.

Similarly, there were lows, like when *Kurbaan* failed. It was one of the earlier films that I had produced, and I really liked it but it felt like a personal failure because my instinct had failed. The second time it happened was when *Kalank* was released—with investments of passion, love, and money—and it didn't do well. It was rejected from day one, and I could understand why, but it just breaks one's heart to see such a product of love fail. When other films failed at Dharma, I had an instinct. I'd walk out of an edit room and tell everyone it's great because I need to boost the morale of my team but I never lie to the filmmaker—even if I lie to all the others involved.

What is it that you look at when you're deciding on a movie to finance—is it the actor, the genre, the script?

It's a combination of two things. First, the digital revolution has divided genres, so certain genres absolutely should not be theatrical. For example: Slice of life, human dramas, and romantic love stories, like *Ek Main Aur Ek Tu, Salaam Namaste* are the kinds that are now operating only digitally as opposed to *Kabir Singh* which is a dramatic love story and can have a theatrical angle. Certain genres will just not work unless you have a big theatrical experience.

Take horror comedies for example; comedies and horror alone might not work but horror-comedy is now a big genre. Similarly, big ones like *Dhoom*, *Pathaan*, *War,* and then more specifically the big spectacles, like *Baahubali*, *RRR*, *KGF,* and *Pushpa* that are rooted in India. Then there are the outliers, the ones that will not conform to my theories here but break through the theatres, like *Kantara* which got a footfall similar to *KGF* in Karnataka. It's huge because the cost to profit on *Kantara* is massive and I would only compare *Kantara's* cost-to-profit to a film released in the '70s called *Jai Santoshi Maa*, which had come very close to the business of *Sholay*. In my knowledge, *Kantara* was made in ₹15 or ₹18 crore, and the worldwide return could be touching ₹1,000 crore.

If a consumer pays ₹100 for a ticket, how is that ₹100 divided amongst the actors, the directors, the producer, and the theatre?

Unfortunately, a good part of that goes to the movie stars, which should not be the case, because not every movie star can open a film at every given point of time, but you're paying them the top dollar. So, if it's a big director, then 50% to the star, 30% to the director, and the rest goes to the technical teams and other contributors. Now, there's a little more that goes to the writer but the producers are the last people to make money.

Is that the same in the West as well?

No, the superstar is dead in the West.

But even in India, the evolution of the superstar is not looking too promising.

I don't think any of our new generation movie stars can have the aura and magic of Shah Rukh Khan, Salman Khan, Aamir Khan, Amitabh Bachchan, Akshay Kumar, Ajay Devgn, Hrithik Roshan—they were truly 'The Last of the Mohicans'. Today's stars will be relevant and famous, but fame and superstardom are two totally different things. Anybody can become famous but are you a superstar that people are standing in queues for? That is not happening anymore.

Can a movie earn good money despite being a flop; and similarly, not earn good money despite being a hit?

The essence is to focus on how economically driven the movie is. A film could be a flop and make money if you've managed to keep your costs in control. Similarly, you could make a massive movie, which makes a massive number, but you have spent so much money that you have to cover your costs first. So, cost optimization is more important. Yash Raj Chopra once said, 'A film never fails, a budget does.'

> *A film could be a flop and still make money if you've managed to keep your costs in control.*

If an entrepreneur—who has no background in cinema, and is not an actor—wants to break through in the business of cinema, what are the existing opportunities?

There have been some inspiring success stories like that of Guneet Monga, who founded Sikhya Entertainment. She's come up the tough way and initially knew no one in the industry. She worked with Anurag Kashyap and some others before she made *The Lunchbox* which garnered a lot of international love. Sikhya Entertainment remains one example of a startup breakthrough. It's rare, difficult, and certainly not a cakewalk.

If one doesn't want to be a filmmaker, but still wants to be in the industry as a startup, what are some verticals to explore?

If you do not want to fund or produce a film, and if you seek advice from the right people and hire the right ones then you can have a full-fledged PR agency or a startup that makes marketing posters. Even that requires one to understand the DNA of the film industry and how it works in its true nature.

If you have a tech-inclined mindset then exploring VFX (visual effects) can be great. It is such a big component that it only requires people who have excellent technical abilities.

Is there a shortage of technical manpower? If a VFX company was to be established in this day and age, would it thrive?

Yes, absolutely. If a VFX company were to be established today, it could do well, but it would also need some relationship-building. In that scenario, it's helpful to have an insider from the industry on board with you—whom people recognize and whose calls they pick up. Ideally, you might have the best lot, but if you're not able to reach out to people, then the point goes missing.

Are there any needs to hire MBA graduates, or engineers in the film industry? Do you hire either of these?

Absolutely! In my office out of our strength of 400 or 500, we have about 100 MBAs—in legal departments, and finance departments, our CEO and CFO are also MBA graduates.

We hear about Netflix doing data crunching, and that's how they arrive at a consensus on which movies to make and whom to cast. Is there a similar activity you carry out regarding data crunching?

I've always been a very firm believer in research when a film is made. However, I am also a firm believer that screenplays and songs have to be instinct-driven and I don't want them to become mechanical in the process. It's a form of expression and a creative art form but when the film is ready—because it's for an audience—that's when one must treat it like selling a product. But as a thumb rule, first, go by your gut instinct, don't put everything to research. Then show it to an organization like Yuvaa that does research screenings. What they do is provide feedback, scores, and recommendations, and after incorporating their feedback and altering the movies slightly, they have worked well for us.

If you had to design a course on the business of Indian cinema, what would the curriculum look like and what are some titles you'd go with?

Firstly, to understand the business, it's important to understand the context it is set in—the timelines and the essence of that history. The first topic would be the history of Indian cinema, even if it is covered only briefly. I'd love for students to dive deep into the cinema of the 1950s—typically called the Guru Dutt era—and onwards. It was the time when intensity and the extent of social issues were at their peak. India had recently got its independence and there was a delayed reaction in cinema. Then, the 1960s came—the famous *YaaHoo* phase of Shammi Kapoor—where movies were shot at popular hill stations. The plots would have a resolved, happy ending, without many dramatic angles to it. Then came the Emergency, which caused angst in the common man, and Salim–Javed created the idea of the 'angry young man' with their writings. In this era, Amitabh Bachchan ruled, being the face of that 'angry young man'. It was then that 'action' as an act and genre emerged for the first time which also resulted in a lot of action in Telugu and Tamil cinema. The idea of the 'hero' started in the 1970s while the 1980s went into the remakes of South Indian films. The 1990s brought back love, crushing action to the core, as can be witnessed with *Dilwale Dulhania Le Jayenge, Hum Aapke Hain Kaun,* and *Kuch Kuch Hota Hai.* It was a fine blend of romance, love, and globalization that created Shah Rukh Khan. History tells one the order of events.

Then comes the business segment and I'd like to circle back to budgets, recoveries, terms like gross, net, and entertainment charts, understanding what ticket price is and what eventually comes home as a part of the profit. Then we move on to genres to understand what's working and what's not working, and to the big divide of digital versus theatrical, revenue streams, and negotiations.

What is the hardest deal that you had to negotiate and who is more difficult to negotiate with—distributor or actor?

All deals are tough because everybody walks in with their defenses up. One would like to get the top dollar, but the other would not want to give in. So you settle in between. Actors are more difficult because they come with delusions of their own sometimes, but negotiation is part of the process. Being a filmmaker, we need to be polite and firm, to justify the numbers the deal is being made on. Often, the actors' management companies are even more difficult to crack, and having a company of my own, I tell people that you must work for the producer—who is reasonable and offers you data and analysis—not the actor.

We have a trend of using case studies as a way of teaching at Masters' Union. If you were to use a movie's case study to teach the following, which movies would they be:

1. **Marketing:**
    PK, 3 Idiots, and *Dangal* because Aamir Khan uses really creative devices to market the films he works on.

2. **Branding and Positioning:**
   Branding often happens as a default. Take *Kabhi Khushi Kabhi Gham*—it suddenly became 'K3G' and it has stuck with people. Similarly, Namrata Joshi, who writes for *Outlook* magazine, once wrote 'The KJo Effect' in one of her articles and since then Karan Johar has become KJo. That is the power of one article, and one tagline sometimes. Hence, the result of 'branding' is not always organic. It just happens like magic.

3. **Budgeting:**
   Kantara

4. **Risk Taking:**
   Brahmastra involved massive risks. Huge budget. Crazy idea. I was so nervous that I was getting defensive over that film. With so much praise, criticism, and opinions flung around, and Ayan trying to deliver the film, the stress was at an all-time high.

5. **Strategy:**
   KGF demonstrates great strategy, especially the decision to make it into two films. Similarly, *Pushpa* was a great strategy too.

If you had to bring in masters from the cinema industry to come and give guest lectures as part of your course. Who would you call for the following?

1. **Movie Promotions:**
   I'd call myself for that!

2. **Data:**
   Ormax or an informal chat with the gentleman who runs Box Office India.

3. **Negotiating Fees:**
   Bhushan Kumar, since he has struck so many deals.

If Bollywood was a startup, who would you have as the following?

1. **CEO:** Shah Rukh Khan
2. **CFO:** Akshay Kumar
3. **CMO:** Myself!
4. **CTO:** Again, Shah Rukh Khan, he has a great technical mind.
5. **CHRO:** Can't think of anyone but myself!

Let's talk about the future of cinema and where we are headed: If you had ₹100 crore to invest, how would you split it between Dharma, your traditional business; and Dharmatics, your OTT initiative?

In present times, it would be ₹60 crore to Dharma and ₹40 crore to Dharmatic. But since digital is a huge component now and comes with assured money back, possibly in four years, it could be ₹60 crore to Dharmatic and ₹40 crore to Dharma. While my heart lies in filmmaking and I would hope to give Dharma ₹80 crore, that's not the case. Modularity will be sixty-forty, eventually tilted on one of the sides.

If we manage to be successful, then the tilt will be towards Dharmatic but if we manage to release movies like *Pushpa* and *KGF*, with one *Kantara* thrown in—then my plan would be to move to the mountains and wave from there.

According to a report, the Telugu film industry had a 28% market share in terms of revenues while the Hindi film industry's share stood at 27%. If you had ₹100 crore to invest again, how would you split it between Bollywood versus the rest?

It becomes a hypothetical question because I'm not equipped to make a Telugu film. The Telugu audiences are indeed much more faithful to their movie stars and turn up in huge numbers to support them. The numbers from North America and the Middle East are massive. I would obviously invest in Telugu films if I was just a filmmaker who didn't have a preference of sorts. But my heart lies in Hindi cinema.

To answer as a business person, however, Telugu cinema is a far more lucrative industry. So, from ₹100 crore, it would be a solid sixty-forty split, from a strict business and outsider's point of view.

Are there any competitors or trends that keep you up at night?

What keeps me up is that a lot of us have lost our core conviction. When I wrote *Kuch Kuch Hota Hai*, its plot line revolved around a child who was reading those eight letters left by her mother before she passed away. That was the conviction. I have two six-year-old kids. They aren't reading any letters. The way the college in that movie looked was just conviction. I insisted on that summer camp bit in the film, which has no roots in our society. At that time, everything was not logical. We have lost our conviction in Hindi cinema because we started worrying too much about the applause and praise on social media, including me, especially about what the critics have to say.

What keeps me up is that a lot of us have lost our core conviction.

***Brahmastra* had a lot of conviction.**

Yes, it did, and that's why it earned the kind of money it did. The reviews were not good at all but the conviction worked.

What do you think it will take for India to produce its *Avatar*, *Harry Potter* franchise, or *Game of Thrones*?

We are not behind in terms of storytelling, vision, or even human resources. We have that in our Indian cinema, texture, and DNA. What we don't have is the exhibition. We don't have screens. We have about 10,000 screens and we're competing with 1,00,000 screens. The world is ready to watch *Avatar* but we don't have that kind of screen count. The moment we have a cinema every square kilometre or every two kilometres in our country, the sky's the limit. There are so many people who still don't have access to cinema screens.

If there was a Hindi or a Kannada movie dubbed in English, do you think it would be a global sensation?

RRR is a great example. It caused such a massive stir with the media in North America, to the extent that it's a Golden Globe nominee-nominee for the Best Motion Picture: Non-English Language. Then Rajamouli Sir won the Critics' Choice Award for the Best Foreign Language Film.

We're already nearly there.

Is there money in dubbed films?

The money is there but we have just one Rajamouli Sir. That's the limiting factor.

Will you ever want to sell Dharma Studios?

I'm not even close to selling it but I was close to doing it about five or seven years ago. At one point, emotional ideologies were clouding my mind—like my father built this brand and so on. But in the pragmatic world, if we need to raise money or sell a stake in our enterprise, it's only to enhance the infrastructure of our company, and not for any personal gains. Apoorva and I have discussed this at length. I need to make my company bigger and the only way I can do it is if I have more money to take more and more chances, and sensibly invest that money in the infrastructure of Dharma Productions and Dharmatic Entertainment.

Even after three decades in the industry, what keeps you motivated—is it the awards, the revenue, or are you just enjoying the process and having fun?

I'm having a lot of fun. I love it. But what I am still looking for is the lovely blockbuster number. I want to wake up to those big numbers. That still drives me. It's like a report card and one wants all A+ across.

You just don't want to be happy with Bs and Cs. I've always been so enamoured with the box office only because it's such a validation. It's the screaming out-loud audience, saying we love your work and your film. That's what you want.

> *What I am still looking for is the lovely blockbuster number. I want to wake up to those big numbers. That still drives me. It's like a report card and one wants all A+ across.*

There would be many MBA students who might read this conversation. What is your final message to them?

I know many people who, for various reasons, have taken up academic decisions, based on peer, societal, or family pressures because everybody wants them to have a stable job. There are those who have MBAs and financial degrees, but they have creative drives. To them, I'll say that the entertainment industry awaits your minds because you're a strong balance of academia and passion, and that's what I am always seeking as a filmmaker. So if you are one of those people who have a creative bent of mind but have pursued an academic path, that doesn't mean the entertainment industry is closed for you. It just means that you have to be more daring with your choices.

The only way you can learn to make films is by making films and similarly, the only way to learn business is by actually getting on and doing it.

Malika & Mohit Sadani

the moms co

The Moms Co was established in 2016 and offers 100% natural and toxin-free products with over thirty ranges including pregnancy care, baby care, face care, hair care, and more.

Malika, for whom launching The Moms Co stemmed out of a personal concern, has been the solid brains behind the operations of the brand. She pursued her MBA from Welingkar and is one of the 40 under 40 entrepreneurs awarded by Business World. Her grit, passion, and need for safe products for moms and babies led her to launch the brand with utmost honesty and transparency.

Mohit, who joined the rocket ship later, had faith in Malika's grit. He pursued his MBA from IIM, Ahmedabad. Mohit comes with rich experience in consulting, consumer goods, and retail companies from McKinsey. He always had an itch to enter entrepreneurship and more specifically e-commerce, seeing the traction it got. With Malika's idea, Mohit got a venture to put his mind behind and together they built a company that is trusted by many.

CHAPTER 6

The 11 p.m. Calls That Built The Moms Co

In conversation with Malika and Mohit Sadani, Founders and CEOs of The Moms Co

In this candid conversation, Malika and Mohit, the faces of The Moms Co discuss entrepreneurship where perseverance, passion, and adaptability are key ingredients. For both of them, the journey of building The Moms Co from an idea into a successful, toxin-free, and natural products brand is as much about personal experiences as it is about market strategy. From Malika's initial challenges of finding safe baby care products to Mohit's deep-rooted passion for entrepreneurship, their story speaks volumes of the highs and lows of growing a business in such a dominated and competitive landscape.

❖❖❖

What were your foundations like—education, family, childhood? Did they influence being an entrepreneur?

Malika: Being an army officer's daughter, my childhood involved moving every two years to a different place. As I grew up, I pursued Electronics as a degree and after finishing that, went on to work at CMS Computers in a management-led role instead of a networking-led role. I did that even though the company was known better for the latter. After that, I worked at ICICI Bank for about three years and thoroughly enjoyed my time there. I was certain that this was what I would be pursuing later in life. As fate would have it, I was expecting my first child, and with Mohit's official transfer to London, we moved there.

As opposed to what many know, The Moms Co was not my first idea. The first idea was to have a creche for children since I noticed a gap in Mumbai after I had moved there after my first child's birth. It didn't work out, but through that, The Moms Co happened. It was a very personal journey of being unable to find products that were toxin-free and safe for kids' skin. The idea got stuck with me and we soon dived right in, regardless of the fact we had never done cosmetology or studied anything in that domain.

Mohit: I grew up in Bahrain, and chose to come back to India in 2000 to pursue my college degree. After that, I worked at TCS (Tata Consultancy Services) for a couple of months and realized that was not a career I wanted to pursue. I studied for CAT and worked at McKinsey for over seven years. Those years proved to be great and gave me an opportunity to strengthen my avenues for consumer goods, retail, organizations, etc. Back in 2014, I realized that the real revolution was happening in e-commerce, so with that intent, I joined Snapdeal and led their growth and strategy segment for a year and a half. During that time, Malika came with her pain points and effectively hired me for my knowledge of social media and e-commerce to launch a brand.

During your college days, did you know that you were trudging yourselves towards entrepreneurship?

Malika: I never thought I'd become an entrepreneur; my journey with motherhood led me to this.

Mohit: I, however, always knew I would become an entrepreneur. I was quite passionate about this even during my days in Bahrain where I initiated a short venture around lending books which didn't work well eventually. Even later, I always had half a foot in entrepreneurship at all points in time.

What are some hardships of entrepreneurship that many don't know about?

Mohit: How an entrepreneur experiences the many aspects of life is different. When you have a steady job, and there are bad days, your emotions fluctuate a bit; upon having a child and seeing them sick, your emotions further start escalating like a wave, but when you have a business to run, and the PR and funding are not in your favour, it's a full-blown hurricane. Everything inside you shifts. The highs in entrepreneurship can feel very high, the lows will be the lowest. When I meet founders now, I simply tell them that the biggest strength you need is emotional resilience. Because you have to be able to not get impacted by that as much.

The biggest strength you need as a founder is emotional resilience.

What was the genesis of your idea to play as another D2C (direct-to-consumer) player among the big and established giants like Johnson & Johnson, Dabur, Himalaya, etc? What gave you the muscle to fight with those?

Malika: First, we were naïve. Second, we thought what have we got to lose except money, which we were sure would come back. We gave ourselves three years to gauge our business's progress and one always knows which direction their business is going in, so honesty was a necessity at that juncture. One needs to commit themselves to the business they are doing and if they do well, that is great. If they don't, then circle back on what's going wrong and why is it that your business is stuck and not moving.

The last leg was to go back and take up a job, in case we reach the minimum bank balance that we had in mind. At one point, the worry hits whether employers will take us as a failure but we gave ourselves enough confidence that we will go back richer with more knowledge, something our peers might not have.

What was the inception of The Moms Co like? You started with fewer products and now have expanded to such huge numbers.

Malika: The original model was to launch products for babies but as we got mentorship from industry leaders, we switched to a rather unoccupied parallel path. The path was to first target women who were pregnant and then launch baby products after we had gathered the parents' trust and faith in our range.

One critical aspect of entrepreneurship is that founders need to be very agile. Our brand, which was supposed to be a baby care brand, actually ended up becoming a mom brand, because once the pregnancy products were launched, we were asked, where are the post-pregnancy products for mothers? Products for solving issues like hair fall, muscle recovery, and so on. We first catered to those problems and later launched baby products. Eventually, baby products as a range became a segment but the larger segment stuck with products for new mothers and their needs.

Seems like you were really listening to your consumers and their needs at the time.

Malika: Absolutely! At one point, we were delivering products and taking customer calls even at 11 p.m. We have had some great conversations and insights on how people perceived our brand. We had some of the best takeaways from those conversations. We would even deliver products for babies under their name, to add a tinge of personalization.

Mohit: One time, I interacted with a customer while delivering an order for her in my BMW 3 series, one I had bought with much pride and joy. She was expecting a delivery partner on a bike, and she was stunned to see me in such a car. I spoke to her and understood that she was sending the pregnancy gift box to her sister-in-law in Dubai. It was then that we realized this particular gift box is creating waves and had a massive demand so we doubled down on that.

Did these conversations lead to the creation of formal rules between the two of you and how did you navigate those?

Mohit: We didn't have any formal set rules. Rather, we were driven by our skill sets. While Malika oversaw marketing, product, operations, and brand building, I was in charge of fundraising, hiring, and sales.

Malika: It was great that there were no rules defined from day one. We gradually evolved with our processes and choices around what we liked doing, rather than what we did or did not envision doing.

What was your initial emotional reaction to launching your first products?

Malika: I was devoid of any emotions. I was the same way even after delivering my first child.

Mohit: The moment I held my first daughter I was teary-eyed and said to myself that this amazing miracle wouldn't have existed if it were not for us. Similarly, I felt teary-eyed and grateful while holding the first bottle of the product we launched.

You were having many conversations with mothers, customers, and young kids but who was your key intel generator on the outside?

Malika: We had some intelligent mentors like the global head of Nestle who was based out of Switzerland, and Shripad Nadkarni, who is a marketing genius. They would advise us on potential roadblocks and we would be optimistic that we would not land in one; but eventually, if that happened two months later, we would go to them to seek advice. Much of the intel for a business actually comes from the consumers—how are they responding to the product, what are they liking, what's the next thing they want? Since there are a lot of agencies who help with that, it is not the most difficult part. What is critical, however, is to get intel from people who honestly tell you where they think the lags are, with regards to the culture and the product we are building.

Were you able to build the company culture you had envisioned?

Malika: It was difficult but we eventually did it. We, as founders, followed different work routines so our teams would get emails from me at 2 a.m., and from Mohit at 5 a.m., which made it difficult for them. We didn't realize this was happening until someone walked up to us and asked if this was what we wanted to build. If one wants to talk about work-life balance, it needs to stem from us to set an example. We had to first inculcate that in our own lives and only then would it trickle down to employees. Our culture involved ownership, hustle, and primarily, to have a sense of belonging.

We have had examples of people sacrificing their personal lives to such an extreme extent that we had to make public conversations around it and let them have time with their families. It happened after our employees had shown their vulnerabilities but we had set very clear instructions that such sacrifices cannot be made. Families are important. Through all those conversations, empathy started to kick in massively.

We also got tools in place to equip ourselves with defining a culture. I am a firm believer of the fact that culture is not something that we, as founders, can narrate to people. Culture is what employees narrate when we are not in the room.

Mohit: Culture doesn't build organically. One needs to create it and inculcate it through conversations. The best way to do that is to have stories around the culture we are building. If we are saying that we are honest to our consumers, that needs to start with honesty amongst each other within the company. We'd give examples and narrate stories since humans are storytellers and we naturally gravitate towards stories.

> *Culture is not something that we, as founders, can narrate to people. Culture is what employees narrate when we are not in the room.*

How is your leadership style at work?

Mohit: I was very hands off and I'd allocate tasks to people and trust them to figure those out. If they'd have a roadblock, they'd come back to me and that'd give me a lot of time to get other work done.

Malika: I'd operate slightly differently—I'd have meetings right in the morning and since our team had very experienced people on board, there wasn't much for me to contribute. What I'd do otherwise was understand how I can enable these experts to achieve the next big thing. It could include collaboration between two teams, and aligning the company's vision, product, and process with how they function.

Have you ever fired someone for a silly reason?

Malika: We were actually terrible at firing and often we would push our resources, time, and energy into teaching someone a particular thing.

Mohit: And if they did not have the drive to learn it, it would be a waste of multiple resources at the same time. Which actually helped us in hiring better.

What are some non-negotiables while hiring?

Malika: Lying is a big red flag. If what you have mentioned in your pitch or portfolio doesn't add up while performing reference checks, I will not hire you. Second is skills: I get energized by extremely smart people and if I see it missing at the other end, we might not be able to work together.

Mohit: I believe that you cannot teach or coach the idea of a 'drive'. If a person is fundamentally driven and really wants to achieve in life, they'll do it anyway. I enjoy coaching, teaching, and offering tools to people that help them really achieve what they want, but if they are not driven, you can't do much to change it.

In a remote setup, what would be your advice on managing people, considering the different emotional spaces they are in with different routines?

Malika: Online mode of work didn't work for us for a long time so we had to come back to the offline setup, as soon as we could. However, we conducted one-on-ones with employees to understand their struggles and pain points. Later, as circumstances appeared, we'd have to let people go if they were not serious about their roles or the time they should be investing and working with us. On the opposite end, there were also times when we would stay in touch and understand what was going on in an employee's life and send them food at their place when they'd have none to eat. These small gestures would make a difference but we'd also be strict and make decisions where they were required.

Mohit: Flexibility, which is understood as a great factor in managing time, resources, and money well, can often get assumed as something else when team members don't have clarity on what they are supposed to do on the day they are visiting the office. These scenarios can be easily clarified in an office setup, as everyone is around, but are absolutely difficult to navigate in a remote setup.

How did you validate the market fit for 100% natural and toxin-free products? What made you differentiate between the products you are looking for and not looking for?

Malika: Qualifying natural products wasn't hard because it was defined. Every product that one consumes has a report and a certificate that comes with it which mentions its originality and authenticity. The harder part was defining what we as a brand wanted to stand for and how we ended up saying that we wanted to be natural and toxin-free. There is an entire ecosystem of suppliers and ingredients set up in the market for us to be able to manufacture what we desire. But it stemmed from people gravitating towards safer products and natural ones. These are the two pillars on which we decided to build the product: Safe and natural. Once that was done, it was just about getting experts on board from around the world who could actually formulate the product for us.

Mohit: From a brand perspective, we approached the problem by asking why are moms uncomfortable today. The brands they would go to had been in the market for over a hundred years and it's an obvious factor that they can be trusted. We, as a new brand, pivoted towards the opposite extreme: we overloaded them with information and put a rating chart on the website that showed we were certified by many parameters. The narrative we set was: 'We know you are a mother and are worried about your child and what goes on their skin, and here's what we have.' We'd encourage mothers to look at our packaging that described about the product and build trust for themselves or visit our websites for even more detailed information. Beyond this, if one needs even more information than that, we're here to talk! That was the narrative we were building.

How do you address the challenge of a product succeeding in one market but not fitting well in another? Additionally, before seeking approvals, what factors determine the ideal sample size and the effectiveness of tests and trials?

Malika: We had a team within the company that constantly looked at new products globally and separately within India, both offline and online. Understanding the market gap, if there was one, would help us create a pipeline for new products. The other stream was that our suppliers would keep telling us about the ingredients and options that they go well with. Then we would identify what sits in really well with our brand, and pick up on those products to put them into the development cycles. We would then formulate the product viability by understanding what the product will stand for and its key ingredients. Testing is quite a standardized process across the country and they would ask for a standard sample size which you then provide and they carry out a test for you.

Do 100% natural ingredients mean they are non-harmful?

Malika: Not necessarily. Ingredients could be all-natural, but they could come together to become toxic since some ingredients wouldn't sit well with the other, so the final formula could be unsafe for use. More often than not, natural products, rather than synthetic ones, actually have more issues so it's very important that the entire product is safe.

Were there any products that were manufactured but never made it to market? If so, were they shelved because consumers didn't respond as expected?

Malika: Our products would be tested over nine months after manufacturing so there were none that didn't see the light of the day.

Mohit: But there were some that didn't get a massive response, like our body scrubs, which we launched after COVID, when the wave of self-care had hit the world. They didn't fit well in our narrative of products for mothers and babies.

How did you combat newer brands that were coming in such as Mama Earth which was launched in 2016?

Malika: We had the first movers' advantage in that case and we were clear that other players would keep coming in. We simply focused on our products, what we are offering, and what the company stands for.

Back when you launched, D2C was a relatively new term. Did you ever have second thoughts about not launching this product, especially with a D2C model?

Malika: We didn't have an option of going the retail route as we didn't understand the challenges it came with or have the money to take that road. We were convinced that many consumers are now moving online and we would tap into that. Back then, not many people were sure of entering their bank details on a website to make transactions and buy products. One time, a celebrity, who was one of the first customers, actually enquired if it was safe to put her details on our website.

We couldn't have gone big in the initial days if we had launched through retail. It required heavy distribution, products, and working capital and we didn't have any.

When was it that you decided to raise an amount? What number were you going with and from which partner?

Mohit: It was always about the potential we want to go after. In the first round, our product was ready and we needed funds to market and focus on brand building so we did that. The second time, our e-commerce vertical was stabilized and we wanted to explore retail, so we raised funds to achieve that. It's important to gauge what you will be unlocking with the funds you get and simultaneously keep a check on whether your goals were achieved and potentials were tapped the first time you raised money for a particular segment. Understanding when to raise money is more about a benchmark than a time frame.

Malika: Additionally, there cannot be one linear answer to it as one might also decide to raise funds when they observe their competitors changing gears. It's then you need more marketing, faster growth, etc. which wouldn't be happening if there was no competition.

What did your first round of fundraising look like?

Mohit: The first round we raised was quite difficult to get through, as there was a lot of negative press around startups at the time. We raised about ₹1.15 crore from a group of seven angel investors, a concept that was not as famous back then. With that, we ensured that the brand must be strong enough for mothers to trust us, beyond our focus on quality, content, and the information we put forth. A large chunk of our capital went into getting the name, product, and colours right. That focus helped us get our round of investment which happened a month into our sales. We launched in March 2017 and by April, we had a term sheet from DSG Capital and Saama Capital. They had been looking for a brand in the same space as ours because they had a firm belief this was going to be the next big thing. Over time, we built a deep relationship with them and continued to raise over ₹10 million through our journey of The Moms Co.

As founders, what were the financial metrics that helped you assess the company's growth and the direction it was headed towards?

Mohit: One must look at the financial metrics from two lenses: Performance and potential. Performance comprises analyzing how the company is doing at present, which is to understand brass tax on revenue, cost, EBITDA (Earnings Before Interest, Taxes, Depreciation, and Amortization), and cash flows. Potential means if you have the right tools to scale the business. Understanding what is the repeat rate—at a customer level and separately at a product level—and what the brand health looks like. This further extends to the idea that we are the preferred brand of a consumer. Are we on the right track from a potential perspective, so that we see demand growing and business growing, and also our ability to support it operationally? It was how we judged the collective financial metrics for our business.

Malika: Additionally, in our company, each vertical had three segments they had to focus on: Cost (how are you improving cost structures), profitability (how are you envisioning to eventually contribute to that), and what new are you building (it could be anything under the sun, tech for example).

Should a founder raise before utilizing the cash that is sitting idle with them? Is that a better space to be in while thinking futuristically of the potential?

Malika: Ideally, it's not a better approach. If with the money in hand, you can reach a rather extensive audience and scale, with everything externally working in your favour, then you should not raise funds. One does raise potential and raise early, but not so early that you are unclear of the potential segment you'll be spending in. Push it out as much as you can, but simultaneously, have enough and more run rate for your business to last. Fundraising is not any cakewalk so having a fairly reasonable run rate is important to get the best valuation.

A number game boils down to sales and marketing and it's often said that they are cousins of a brand. Was there a particular campaign that made it big for your topline sales and revenue?

Malika: There was not one but a series of campaigns and marketing that we did throughout, since our category is unique. Trust doesn't get built from one campaign, but is built from a series of actions that you take through small steps to make it big. However, one campaign that attracted attention from even bigger FMCG (Fast-moving consumer goods) brands was the one we did with Kalki Koechlin. It was focused on an age-controlled range. People believed that a narrative such as that should have come from a big FMCG brand, and the celebrity we chose was interesting as well. The narrative that quickly picked up was how we selected ageing as a concern because the campaign revolved around ageless expressions. It hit home for most consumers at that point in time, because what we launched was retinol, but to make it true to the brand, we made a natural alternative to retinol. In that range, from a research perspective, we actually beat the bigger players. The campaign launched in November, and January was when many FMCG CEOs were in the office, building conversations around acquisition.

Mohit: Another campaign that struck chords was around the launch of the baby care segment. About 6,000 people had purchased products from us in one year, and we coded a personalized message. That message mentioned the launch of the baby care range and if the consumer was interested, we'd send them a free sample gift box to take a look. For a long while, both of us just punched those orders at the back end. The extent of word-of-mouth marketing and the positive outlook that generated was great. This is us as a brand saying, 'We know we are an upstart and you've trusted us.'

> *Trust doesn't get built from one campaign; but is built from a series of actions that you take throughout your small steps to make it big.*

What was the defining experience that pushed you past the threshold and led to making one of the largest exits in India?

Mohit: Every step through the acquisition unfolded with a different approach tailored to the unique partner who approached us. It was many steps along the way. With FMCG companies, the narrative revolved around retail presence and higher sales. Pharmaceutical companies looked at us with a different lens: they recognized our potential in the pharma space, having natural and toxin-free products that would be perfect for doctors to prescribe to the patients. Their large network in the healthcare sphere created a synergy that blended well with our approach.

Good Glamm, where the deal actually happened, had a strong link of content and commerce. The Moms Co was to add a sharp segment that merged well with their existing content approach, something to complement their ecosystem. Despite the many varied approaches, the common thread was our sharp, non-competing brand identity, our proven track record, and the untapped potential each acquirer saw in scaling us further.

Was there a vision for the exit?

Mohit: We always wanted The Moms Co to be a number three brand globally. To reach there we'd need a global presence or the ability to build it ourselves, good scope for retail, and access to multiple languages which meant different teams in different places. It then boiled down to the question: With this vision in place, do we want to spend the time, energy, and money it needs and spend two to three decades building that or should we partner with someone to try and do it in the next five years? We decided that for that speed and the accelerated potential of doing it in five years felt exciting from a brand perspective.

What was your emotional response like when the acquisition was going on?

Mohit: The rather difficult part was before the acquisition; to come on the same page and decide that we should be selling the company. Once the acquisition happened, it felt like a switch; like we have to entrust our child with someone else now and we will not have as important a voice in the room as we previously did. Officially, on paper, we decided to take about two years to fully transition and handover but it got done eight months before that timeframe. The best piece of advice that we got, was that once you've handed over the business, you have to ensure that the transition happens as quickly and seamlessly as possible as it's best for everybody.

Are there any decisions which, if you had taken differently, would have changed the narrative of The Moms Co?

Mohit: Not really; we're happy with how things have panned out for us. Of course, there would be minor regrets like retaining some great potential and people with us and maybe that would have escalated us to something bigger but overall, it's a good space to be in.

Malika: There was a VC who once told me how he doesn't invest in first-time founders, as first-time launches are considered the founders' learning experience. It was true since establishing something for the first time brings with it inexperience and lack of clarity on where to spend money and how it's important to have people on board who come with experience and specializations. The next time I have a venture of my own, I'd be mindful of these critical aspects of a business.

You cannot have your foot in multiple doors like managing people, marketing, branding, product, and sales while simultaneously getting your product right. You'd still make the same mistakes but the allocation of the right people for the right job makes it better.

What were some momentous early failures or successes of The Moms Co?

Malika: We learned the hard saying that not every product is going to be a success and that happened with one product of ours; a tea range that was very expensive for the market. The consumers pushed it back considering the price point, and we kept advertising and putting money into it without hearing the customer feedback. That was one failure we should have shut early on.

Mohit: The successful moments, however, kept us awake and excited. For example, the time a woman called us late one night to get her order expedited and wanted delivery the next day. We obliged but also asked her what the urgency was. It was then she said she was on her way to the hospital to give birth and she needed the gift for her child as soon as possible! It was a moment of pride and joy together. Another time was when a woman was on a hospital bed, and she was complimented by the nursing staff on how her belly didn't have any stretch marks. She profusely thanked us in her email as she had used one of our products. Stories such as these would make our day!

What is one area you've improved in and one where you still struggle?

Malika: I didn't know I had a people bone but I learned it through the course of running The Moms Co. There was a saying in our office that my mood, whether it was good or bad, dictated the mood around the office. More often than not, it was the stress encircling the business that would put me on edge. It's true that businesses get created when the times are boring in the office: neither too high nor too low.

Have you ever thought of getting into the unicorn race?

Malika: Always. In our case, however, we realized that for this to become a unicorn, we'd have to spend decades and we were better off selling it.

If given a chance to acquire any of your competitors, who would that be?

Malika: I would acquire mCaffeine because they are a very strong brand with an interesting team.

Mohit: I wouldn't acquire anyone for one simple reason. Now that we can't compete and are friends with our competitors, it's clear how tightly integrated their personal nuances are with that of the company's culture and brand they are building. It's easier to start afresh than acquiring.

If given the chance, would you have chosen to grow without raising funds and continue as you were? Many new-age entrepreneurs today are opting for this path.

Malika: The first time around, we couldn't have done it without raising funds. The Moms Co wouldn't have been what it is today without the funds we got. Raising funds allows you to reduce a period by almost ten times. Funds allow you to put out the advertising, hire talent, and set up an infrastructure, which would be very difficult to do without the money. Hiring talent is quite expensive and not just that, they wouldn't come on board if a startup is not funded. It happens because of a clear assumption that in family-owned businesses with no investors, the founders get a final say and that can be a challenge sometimes.

What is the first step you would take when you have an idea that you want to make a business out of?

Malika: It's very subjective but in our case, we wanted to build a product, a physical one and our exercise went into figuring out how to create that product, and what is the problem we aim to solve. Is the problem large enough that we can base a business on it and expand eventually? Another critical aspect is, do we actually like creating the product because without the enjoyment part, it's not going to work out. Understanding what it takes to make a safe product, we reached out to toxicologists in Singapore and other bigger conglomerates to understand their processes better. We then got in touch with regulatory personnel who helped us in understanding the measures we should be taking care of while building a product. After extensive research, if you find it viable then move ahead with the launch.

Mohit: A common belief that founders build their businesses on, if we are facing a problem, then others might be too. But understanding what it is the consumers are ready to pay for, beyond your personal choices, preferences, and biases is critical.

J.P.Morgan

Kaustubh Kulkarni

Kaustubh is the Senior Country Officer at J.P.Morgan India and Vice Chairman for J.P.Morgan Asia Pacific. His association with J.P.Morgan started in 1997, and he has led critical sectors such as FIG, TMT, digital healthcare, real estate and infrastructure conglomerates, and financial sponsors.

His deep understanding of India's evolving economy and his philosophy—viewing himself as a salesperson at the core—has shaped his ability to drive meaningful engagement with clients and stakeholders, contributing to J.P.Morgan's continued success in one of the world's most dynamic markets.

CHAPTER 7

The Salesman's Mindset: Building Relationships and Driving Growth

In conversation with Kaustubh Kulkarni, Senior Country Officer and Vice Chairman of J.P.Morgan India

---

In this insightful conversation, Kaustubh Kulkarni draws on his two decades of experience to share his vision for India's economic future. He delves deeper into J.P.Morgan's strategic approach and emphasizes the impact of ambition and collaboration on achieving success.

As a key leader in J.P.Morgan's financial segment, he reflects on his perspectives on bonds, equity, leadership, strategy, and navigating India's dynamic business landscape.

❖❖❖

Twenty-eight years is a long time to be in a company. What keeps you motivated?

My journey of twenty-eight years has been primarily driven by a single motive: Keeping things as simple as possible. I have approached challenges by understanding the core problem and the available opportunities. The key is to have a vision to understand the elements of the problems and the opportunities early on.

It starts with mapping out the clients and gauging situations where some of these problems and opportunities might arise. Our observation is that if you can connect with the counterparty—whether it's people, businesses, or other stakeholders—the focus shifts towards collaboration, which then helps in solving problems better. It's about identifying the issue, aligning efforts, and crafting the best possible solution together.

I have worked in different leadership roles through the years. From my time outside India, where I oversaw India and Asia Pacific till today, a common element for me has been 'problem identification'. The bigger the problem, the bigger the opportunity and bigger the importance of achieving that outcome. In the financial services sector, the outcome of what one does has a substantial impact on one's clients. One simply needs to keep adapting themselves to think about the future. Our approach has been about positioning ourselves strategically—utilizing resources, investing time, capital, and efforts—in one direction and then staying fully committed.

Can you share an example to help us understand the situation more cohesively?

When we talk about a company's structure, equity often takes the spotlight—market capital, pricing, valuation. But beneath that lies several stakeholders that you will look at most of the time. Let's consider two credit-related cases from the Indian context, involving major corporations with high credit. These weren't small companies but major ones in this context, and they believed they had solutions to deal with liabilities, but we offered to take a look at their solutions and dug deeper.

Discussions began a year in advance, and we concluded that our plans were sound. We also informed the stakeholders that we are being very conservative. In any financial services business, it's critical to understand and remember who your client is and who has a better advantage on the inside.

Your stakeholder could be speaking with ten of your competitors or could have insights from across the board, so you need to understand where your input stands. That's when judgement and experience come in handy. To have the ability to read the situation and inform the client that there is a small chance that this may not get played the way it is, is important. Fast forward three months before the date, we realized there was a problem—we had certain premises and setups that didn't work in our favour at the last minute, and minds were changed.

In the financial services sector, till the time the money is not in, nothing is final. So, we started aligning all our efforts and putting most of our resources into getting a particular task done by a set date. Commonly, in both the cases, if it doesn't happen, the cascading impact of this problem is you have a default of about $4 or $5 billion across the financial system, which is a nightmare for the banking system.

J.P.Morgan was the only entity that was at the core trying to find a solution and implement it. People didn't have a clue as to what the solution was or how it was going to be implemented. They do not fully appreciate the criticality of it because the moment anybody else knows that it is significant to you, several pounds of flesh will be taken away, and the solution may not even work. The bottom line is that in J.P.Morgan's capital market business, one needs to have a very precise sharpshooter mindset. You are shooting from a very long range.

There are several variables that you could reflect on, and you must time all of it perfectly. You need to have the right bullet for the right target, and you need to hit it right in one single chance. The mindset for me and my company is that if you start one thing, you have to finish it and not stop thinking about all the resulting options. The worst outcome is starting something you cannot finish.

> *The mindset for me and my company is that if you start one thing, you have to finish it and not stop thinking about all the resulting options.*

Moving on to the shareholder activism angle, there are several public situations that we have been involved in, and many of them are still live or being played in some form and manner. In our business, it is a fun collaboration if you are not in the driver's seat because the client is in that seat and is driving very fast with interesting twists and turns. The building blocks of this discussion or this engagement are very similar to interpersonal trust, which is built between the two parties.

The moment your client believes that your interest is different from their interest, then they will look into maximizing their objectives, and you will be left to bring an outcome. The moment the client believes that you are also going to solve for the outcome and with common interests, then it is a win-win situation.

How have you developed the muscle of conviction for yourself and for your team?

In the world of finance, there is no guarantee of being right—no matter which company you represent or who you are. The market is a great leveler, and it will test you every single day. To begin with, one must get rid of this ego that you need to be right and the other person needs to be either less right or wrong. That mindset of not being adamant is something you can gain only through engagements and interactions with the clients. For a company that's been established for over twenty or thirty years and has witnessed many situations, to suddenly trust an individual or a company who is an outsider is an important call. One has to live with the consequences you bring to the table, so trust is something one needs to earn. You have to invest a lot of time and engagement, and it never is a one-person job. Some of the smartest people around value the intent, integrity, and intellect of the counterparty with whom they are interacting. While in your mind, it could be a short haul, but in my experience, at J.P.Morgan, we have been associated with clients for over twenty, twenty-five years. We have been able to build our engagement because we have evolved and continue to stay relevant. In financial investments and personal spheres of life, the compounding of engagement and relationship pays enormous dividends over time. Even in client engagements, a deepening of your relationships over a long time always results in materially greater payoffs. These benefits grow as the relationship continues to build. However, you need to match the pace of this growth. This brings us back to the first interactions: Problems, opportunities, and solutions.

Sales is often perceived as a less aspirational role and segment for post-MBA careers. However, your success in building strong relationships with clients and government stakeholders has been highlighted as pivotal to your leadership journey. Could you elaborate on how these relationships have directly contributed to your career growth and why it is important?

I've always thought of myself as a salesperson, regardless of what my role is titled. Going back to the basics: I think you are always either selling something or making something. At the core, if you are not able to sell your value proposition, be it in investment banking, corporate banking, asset management, or wealth management, then essentially, it's over. The moment you're asking somebody to part with something, then you must understand what is the motivation for the counterparty to do that. Dig down to the basics of that.

The two essentials are time and money. Whichever businesses you go to will have either of them as their core fundamentals. The best impact is if people have been able to part their time with me, and I've been able to learn something that has allowed me to make money. That is special. Nobody can give you money, but they can offer you ideas, and ideas can only come when somebody is spending their time. That engagement of time is a sales effort because somebody is investing in one way or the other.

If you're not doing that, then you're exceptional in thinking of new ideas and putting those new ideas into creating new companies, which is the essence of 'making'. It could be creating new products, software and then you can put the sales part to someone whose core skill set is that. If you speak to the largest number of managers of money in the world and ask where they spend a large portion of their time? They're selling their efforts and time to market their performance to the investors so that they can raise more money, which is also a way of selling. Ultimately, if you're not good at that and not good at convincing people, performance only works up to a point, but ultimately, you need to work on either of the two—making something or selling something.

What are some of your leadership mantras that have helped you in the ups and downs of life?

For me, being present is paramount. One needs to understand what's happening in a particular situation. You may have done tons of preparation with your team, but in the flash of a moment, while you are engaging, something might click in your mind, and you go back to the drawing board.

First, being objective—looking at information ruthlessly, brutally, and objectively at any point in time—is important. Secondly, getting to know and understanding what you previously didn't know is important because that may impact the outcome you'll get. Eventually, knowledge and insights are critical, and having good judgement on which solution is likely to work is the third important thing.

I like to keep the whole narrative of any conversation as simple as possible, regardless of the complex problem statement. If we cannot break it down into digestible inputs of information and action-oriented pieces for either my team or my client, then it doesn't work. Surround yourself with exceptional people and exceptional talent. Work with your team and understand the skill set of each person in your team to see how you can give them brutally honest feedback on what they need to do better. I've witnessed remarkable transformations in people who, from not being optimal performers, became the best ones in three years. It happened because we didn't give up, and we observed that either motivation, synergy, or input was missing, and we worked to fix that. The financial services business is all about people. One must give themselves the best team they can engage and enjoy working with.

What do you look for while building your teams and hiring people?

Some qualities that take precedence are the intent and desire to learn, the effort and intensity one puts in their work, and presenting things with integrity, objectivity, honesty, and something very fundamental but equally substantial: Common sense. I often visit college campuses, and I ask very basic questions that involve common sense, only to realize that students have not dug the problems deeper. Often, their knowledge is surface level. After a couple of questions, I see fumbling and shaking hands, and it's clear that they have not put in the effort. What we are looking for is people who take great pride in their work, who have really done what they claim they have done, and who generally have a good ability to work as a team member because our business is not about individual superstars. We want people who can work extremely well with each other, are hungry, and aspirational.

What is your perspective on The India Story? What about it excites you the most, and where do you see us headed?

The India Story is outstanding. In the building blocks of any economy, there are many variables, primarily the underlying growth and the population's aspirations. In India, the drive to achieve and contribute is unparalleled. The problems that the world is facing: Cost, inflation, talent, labour availability, productivity, are meaningfully different from the problems and opportunities that Indian companies are facing. And so, India is driven by a collective ambition to achieve and contribute across the many strata of society. We are still in the early phases of that journey where this aspiration will manifest itself into greater demand for consumption, financial services, loans, asset management, etc.

Moreover, the biggest thing that will happen in India is that the 'spend' is going to cascade to a much larger portion of the population, which will create enormous opportunities for us. The digital layer and the information layer that we have are enormously advantageous, based on which new businesses are going to be created and built. I think there is a great opportunity to look at the data stack, technology stack, and information stack that we have to re-imagine the number of businesses, how we can change our existing business, to how others can create new businesses, essentially to solve relevant problems. Therefore, the opportunity is quite immense.

What is J.P.Morgan's strategy right now to leverage the evolving landscape?

Historically, our strategy has been wanting to do more with a lot more companies than what we do currently. Our business has scaled four times more than where we were a few years ago, and we are hoping to move as meaningfully as we can in the next few years. We work with about 800 companies of different sizes now, and in 1998 or 1999 the number was about twenty. The revenue segment, however, is meaningfully different today than it was about twenty years ago. On the corporate centre side, which is J.P.Morgan Corporate Centres, we have a large workforce that does exciting cutting edge development work which is yet another big initiative for J.P.Morgan in India. We expect that as India grows, and domestic companies continue to increase, and more multinational companies continue to scale up their business in India, we will witness J.P.Morgan being an important partner in their journey.

J.P.Morgan is very fortunate to have a leader like you who is driving the company forward at this time.

Leadership is truly a team effort. We are building this business for the future, and we have a great team that we have built. With each of our talents and with the depth of the talent we have, we are fortunate to have built what we have built. There is an enormous amount of planning that goes into creating and building the leadership we have today, and we are almost regimental in our approach to doing that. We thrive to create a strong consistency in our engagement and conversations with clients and performance, which ultimately gives us the endurance, the edge and the advantage in dealing with what is an enormously complex work environment. In India, what you realize is just as everything else: It is really hard to make money. For everything they want to offer, they are willing to entertain you and then willing to pay you. The latter is more difficult.

What does working in the bonds and equity department look like? Where do you see the most exciting opportunities between these two areas?

Since J.P.Morgan is the largest equity and the largest credit house, both are great, considering that both the departments make great revenues. However, both also come with their mindsets. Credit is diligence; it requires business understanding, but from a more downside risk protection perspective to see what can go wrong, and how do you recover. If you have given ₹100 to somebody, how can you still recover your ₹100?

Equity mindset, on the other hand, is about understanding: How can you realistically imagine the upsides for different businesses? How can you grow, and how fast can you do it? That's your thesis. Your mindset, if you're doing equity is quite different from your mindset when you're doing credit, but the rest of this is almost the same. Big hedge funds and big long-term investors are active in both.

The credit market is at least three times larger than the equity market given the volume, size, balance sheets of the companies, etc. Hence, both are equally large businesses, but ultimately, it's a function of your style of excitement.

Kaivalya Vohra

Kaivalya Vohra is the co-founder of Zepto, a quick commerce startup, a Stanford dropout, and a Y Combinator alumni. He is responsible for shaping business strategies and leveraging tech through and through—design of the products, application development, security systems, and more. Kaivalya believes that one must go deep into their expertise to solve real-world problems.

Being the youngest person to feature on the 2024 IIFL Wealth-Hurun India Rich List since 2019, Kaivalya holds a net worth of ₹ 3,600 crore. Zepto is a platform that competes against the conglomerate Tata's BigBasket, Swiggy Instamart, and Blinkit, among others.

CHAPTER 8

How Zepto Delivers in 10 Minutes

In conversation with Kaivalya Vohra, Founder of Zepto

Read through Kaivalya Vohra's entrepreneurial journey of building Zepto, from navigating challenges like competing against larger, more established players to making the tough decision to drop out of college to pursue a business idea. In this conversation, he delves into the nuances of executing innovative ideas, the importance of strategic speed, and decision-making in a fast-moving industry. He also touches on the operational intricacies of running a ten-minute delivery model and the underlying psychology of entrepreneurship and risk.

From the importance of understanding the on-ground challenges faced by delivery partners and engineers to navigating the competitive landscape, he highlights how Zepto prioritizes execution, speed, and quality across its services.

◆◆◆

While Zepto has certainly reached the limelight that it deserved with your's and Aadit's efforts, you have established other ventures before. Can you walk us through that journey and explain how it shaped the path to Zepto's current success?

Aadit Palicha and I are childhood friends and have worked on many ideas to fix our pain points. One time, we made a carpooling app to help students commute to school. It was quite an exciting time for us, as we were young and we brought about a dozen schools on board to use this service. The other time, we created Chrome extensions to help with our daily tasks. One day, during my school years, I was reading my economics textbook, and was very excited about podcasts. That sparked an idea: How interesting would it be if I could listen to my textbook? So, I focused on that idea and built a basic prototype of an image-to-speech concept and made it work.

> *An idea sparked: How interesting would it be if I could listen to my textbook? I focused on that idea and built a basic prototype of an image-to-speech concept and made it work.*

Where did the muscle of problem-solving come from? How did you and Aadit develop that problem-solving dynamic together?

My dad fostered a lot of curiosity in me by asking me random questions about why a certain thing was the way it was. Fundamentally, both Aadit and I had an entrepreneurial bent of mind. It goes back to the time when we observed Uber—the cab service—rising and being at its peak, and that idea amazed us. In the business spectrum, there are two traits: Atoms, the businesses' physical assets and inventory that moves (Amazon and Uber); and bits, the digital SaaS (Software as a Service) version of business. We were more inclined towards the atom side of businesses because we were coding back then, and we realized how people are leveraging technology to make atoms move in the real world. I am not sure where the muscle came from, but the curiosity over ideas has always been there.

Aadit and your friendship has been going strong for more than a decade—how did you maintain your friendship while being business partners? How do you hold yourselves accountable?

Realistically, it's the balance of trust and integrity that takes precedence, even beyond one's tech competencies and business acumen. While the highs are incredibly high, the lows are even lower. If you are partnering with a friend whom you have known for a very long time, you will be transparent about your failures and achievements with them, which is very important in any business.

Since we had worked on smaller projects before, we knew how the other person worked, and we could identify aspects where the other needed some push since this is something we wished to build for several decades now.

Since your educational qualifications are somewhat similar, do your strengths overlap, or do you two complement each other?

They are quite complementary. I am inclined to technical aspects, while Aadit is a great storyteller. So, despite our common inclination towards the business, our specializations are different.

Young entrepreneurs always face a dilemma between starting something of their own and joining an organization that they are excited about. How did you decide to drop out from Stanford University and measure the opportunity cost?

My advice would be to just start, unless Zepto is trying to hire you—in that case, join us. Back when we were in school, our end goal was pretty linear—finish our undergraduate degrees, work at a startup for about two or three years, and eventually start something of our own, raise capital, build teams, and scale it. However, we ended up in a position where we had to decide between finishing the degree or dropping out of college. It was during our gap year that we established KiranaKart, raised capital, went through Y Combinator, then shut KiranaKart, raised capital for Zepto, and launched. By then, we had already signed our term sheets for Series B (a $50 million round). At that stage, we weren't worried about the business shutting down tomorrow. The risk of that happening was practically non-existent.

We realized we had an opportunity to do something now that we had envisioned doing at the age of twenty-seven or twenty-eight. Of course, there was the back and forth of convincing our parents, but eventually, that worked.

Looking at the competitive landscape, Zepto entered the market much later than many other players. Were you worried that the incumbents, who had much deeper pockets than you, might tweak their systems or outpace you?

We were concerned, sure, but none of them solved the problem we did—empty fridges and no solution to quickly stock it up. Many delivery businesses had been around for over ten years, but that gap left room for innovation. As for bigger organizations tweaking their systems to compete, they tend to move slowly. This is true for Zepto, too—the speed at which we are executing today, we might not be able to do that five years later. By the time these large organizations hold meetings, make decisions, and execute, we've already gained a solid head start.

What is your advice on the common worry among budding entrepreneurs about sharing ideas, fearing they might be copied?

It's a natural instinct as an entrepreneur to be concerned about your ideas being copied, but 99% of the outcome that one has is during the 'execution' part. Surely, an idea is important to change gears, but it's the execution that makes things happen. It doesn't matter if many are doing the same business as you; eventually, the determining factor in whether you win or not and whether you build a large business or not, is how well you execute. One example of how capital is not the only aspect of running a business is e-commerce: Amazon, Flipkart, Snapdeal, and ShopClues. Even the latter two had good capital, but the performance and response depended on the best execution among the competitors.

It doesn't matter if many are doing the same business as you; eventually, the determining factor in whether you win or not and whether you built a large business or not, is how well you execute.

Zepto's model is very clear: Ten-minute delivery. But why not a five-minute delivery, or fifteen? What has that journey been like for you?

There was a time we had multiple debates about this—five-, ten-, fifteen-minute delivery, but this was our ballpark. Earlier, at KiranaKart our median time was about forty-five minutes, but for those living closer to the confectionery shops, the time became ten to fifteen minutes, and those were the ones who had the best retention and strong word of mouth publicity. We knew people care about the speed of delivery. Ideally, it takes about ten minutes to walk out of the house and buy something for yourself—that was what we wanted to beat, and hence came the ten-minute delivery model.

On the journey front, we realized soon enough that it is a very complicated business—supply chain and retail-wise. Aadit and I were clueless about how to actually build a brand and how to figure out the supply chain. Around March or April of 2021, we raised Series A funding for Zepto and hired talent from MNCs (multinational corporations), as we didn't want to put our time into figuring everything out ourselves. That gave us a head start and allowed us to get things right in the first attempt.

Did you guys face a challenge in 2021 when there was a lot of funding happening in the country across business models? If you did, how did you overcome that?

Our current CCO was living in Bengaluru, overseeing the grocery segment for a big conglomerate. We had just raised funding back then and were ready to hire without even having a name for our company. We reached out to him—asked him to move cities, sacrifice the comfortable life and build this company with us—and his first comment was 'You guys are crazy', but many tough chances later, he came on board.

It was difficult to convince people back then—for instance, my mother, who lived in a high-street bustling neighbourhood of Mumbai, told me that there was no way I could get my groceries delivered in under ten minutes, looking at the realistic traffic circumstances. But it was our craziness and passion that enabled us to build this as quickly as we did.

What goes behind making the ten-minute deliveries happen? What are the challenges you face, and how do you work around them?

Network design—which essentially means where to establish a particular warehouse—is one of the critical aspects of our business model. By the time you are making a payment to place an order, the vehicle is already on the go to deliver within ten minutes. Ideally, we cannot open too many warehouses around the block considering the cost effectiveness, but at the same time, we need to be careful of how we are measuring our network design. Once that is done, we have planogramming—a concept in retail that helps us in shelving commodities, right from the entry gate to the exit point. So, if most orders have common SKUs (stock-keeping units), then planogramming helps us identify if the packer can have a shortcut to packing your order through the entire warehouse. Using a handheld device that has a barcode scanner at the top, the packer gets navigated to where each item is placed in the warehouse and packs it accordingly. It takes about a minute to pack everything that has been ordered and hand it over to the delivery person—the process is that meticulous.

What does a typical Zepto order look like: Category and units wise?

50% of our business is a mix of fruits and vegetables, dairy, and bakery products. In fact, we call it the hot POT at Zepto. Our three highest selling products are potatoes, onions, and tomatoes, and that is like the Holy Grail. The other half of our business consists of cooking essentials, munchies, and home and personal care products, among many other things. In Mumbai, we have Zepto Café, which delivers quick snacks like coffee, tea, samosas, and so on—and we have seen a good response to that. People tend to order that along with their usual grocery order, which is great.

What was your experience at Y Combinator (YC) like?

I would recommend YC to anybody who asks for advice since it added a lot of legitimacy to what we were doing back then. Earlier, the mindset was such that if this doesn't work out, we can simply go back to college. But then, things got real; someone had given us a whopping $125,000 to build this business.

That, coupled with the intensity and rigour of the program, which ran for twelve weeks where each week you're interacting with sharp-minded people, was mind-blowing. One of our group partners was Tim Brady, the first employee at Yahoo, who, through the dot com crash, saw the many downfalls and uphill battles of Yahoo. To have access to that knowledge and experience is great because they help you with all the questions you have and the advice you need, ultimately helping you build your business. Other times, there were weekly sessions where external founders would come in for AMA (ask me anything) sessions.

Beyond accessibility to knowledge, the idea of accountability was even better. Someone like Tim asks you week on week about your progress, and since you're in a group of about five or six different companies, you have a drive inside you that doesn't want others to get ahead of you. So the accountability aspect truly pushes you forward in your way.

It's brilliant because the progress that each company makes in those twelve weeks is quite dramatic. Lastly, YC makes fundraising relatively easier. We would have followed the same process and made the same mistakes, but YC helped us compress the company-building process from one or two years into three months.

Can you walk us through your fundraising journey, especially since you were young founders, were very late in the market, and it was a crowded market. How did YC contribute to that?

We raised a part of the capital during YC, but that was for a different business, KiranaKart. By the end of the YC batch, however, we were clear that the said model would not work—the customer experience wasn't great, and we were not certain of ways to monetize—and realized that we had to do something else. We hadn't thought of a name or how we would do it, but we did have a solid idea for what was later to be called Zepto.

> *Programmes like Y Combinator add a lot of credibility—you'd do the same thing, but people will take you more seriously if you come from such a space.*

Just before Demo Day, we touched base with Suvir Sujan, founder of Nexus, one of India's oldest VC funds. He had experience running multiple big businesses, and he was quite impressed with the execution we had done scaling KiranaKart in the past couple of weeks. Apart from that, he was even more excited about Zepto as a concept and decided to take a chance on us and invested in the idea with about $6.5 million.

YC played a huge part since that brought conviction to him. Eventually, one has to start with fundraising, but the entire process of being a part of YC comes with a ladder of credibility. Hiring one solid person builds credibility, and that's how it went. If we hadn't done these things—KiranaKart, Y Combinator, raised Series A funding—it would have been very difficult to build credibility. As time went on, it became a lot about the business and how well it is, how quickly it is growing, etc. At that point, rather than focusing on having to build this credibility, it just becomes about how well you can execute the model.

What were your factors in bringing a certain investor on board? How do you leverage these investor and board relationships as you grow?

We have been very fortunate with the board that we have. We had a partner, Surbhi, who ran a health tech company for a while. She advised us that by the end of it, it was not actually about running the business but managing the business and board right. We got a lot of advice about being triple sure about the right people and investors we had on board. Every time we raise money, we do reference checks for the investors—the same way we would do while hiring people. Since these investors will be on board with us for about ten years, we need to be sure.

They keep their networks open for us, advise us on our challenges, and stay hands-off on the day-to-day running of the business, which is great for us. Even YC is on our board because they led us through Series C and Series B funding, and they have a growth fund called YC Continuity. We went through YC from January to March in 2021, and in December of the same year, we raised our Series C, $100 million round, which was led by YC Continuity. Within the scope of those twelve months, it was like a full circle moment. Picking and choosing your board members is as important as picking and choosing your co-founders and early hires. It's treated with that same level of gravity.

Since you are also the CTO at Zepto, can you walk us through how you prioritize certain aspects of business and how you decide what to build at what point in time?

Early on, we didn't have any product managers and only ten or fifteen engineers since our hiring was tight. Initially, as a consumer, one needs to be able to browse the product, add to cart and pay, and having some sense of how long it would take is good. Similarly, from the packer's side, they should be able to see what products to pack next. For this, speed was a critical aspect—how quickly this can happen. For delivery, optimizing paths and routing and rider allocation was important—because the whole premise was 'speed'.

Essentially, we focused primarily on the bare minimum that was required to launch. During the launch, there were barely five people in the tech team, but of course, over time, we have grown and now have many verticals across customer support to understand what we can do to make the UX and UI better. Then, our focus was also on the supply chain of products and product management.

We've only recently started quarterly planning for roadmaps and processes. However, the nature of our business means changes are inevitable. Each product manager's scope and outcome is likely to be affected.

What does Zepto's tech infrastructure look like? Scaling without infrastructure breakdowns is a significant achievement. How do you ensure your infrastructure keeps up with growth while maintaining the scale of your business?

One is hiring really talented engineers. Second, as a philosophy, every time you're going to build something, there'll always be five different ways of building it. One is a hacky solution that you could do in two days, but it is not built to last. The other end of the spectrum would be where one can spend six months building this and have it last forever. Then, there are a bunch of solutions somewhere in the middle. This question directs to where one puts themselves on that spectrum. For the agility that we want to maintain, that end of the spectrum where we take six months to build something is just not in the question. There is a common term called tech debt, which is how much tech debt you are okay with having within your system because everything has a shelf life. In my opinion, as long as you're aware of the tech debt, it's fine. When picking a solution, know that it may take two weeks to build, but a year later, you'll need to revisit it. It won't scale long-term. As long as you're taking that call consciously, and you're okay with that to balance agility, it's okay.

For a person in the founding team who is not a person with a tech background, what are ways or what are questions one should ask to be able to identify a talented one?

When I say talented engineers, I'm not talking about technical competence purely. There are a couple of things that are significantly more important than technical competence. One is curiosity, and the other is ownership. Ownership is quite important because we are not an MNC where you're getting a roadmap of steps to follow and things to do. It's largely that you get thrown in the deep end, and you have to figure things out. A lot of people step up, and a lot of people ask to keep throwing problems at them, which they will keep solving. And those are the people who will be getting on calls to solve the issues even before I am aware of it, be it during midnight hours. Those who see the problem first and go deep into understanding the business are the key ones.

> *Ownership and curiosity are two critical qualities to look for while hiring—even beyond the technicalities of their role.*

Our last file engineers have all been on the ground and done deliveries to understand their pain points so that they're able to build software for them. Similarly, our supply chain engineering team, once every couple of months, spends time in our warehouses. They pack orders so that they're able to understand a lot of low-hanging fruit that comes up there. They observe a minor thing, which could be fixed very quickly, so that helps.

It's tricky to be able to judge these aspects in an interview, but one interesting way of judging is going through their resume and understanding the work they must have done on several projects at their past organizations and then trying to double-click into why they did this. Asking why you did this and what happened as a result of that is very insightful. Understanding if this person is going to be afraid to interact with folks in the business and understand business problems is important. Ultimately, engineering products is like problem-solving.

We would over-index on this even more than on technical competence.

Zepto has grown at an incredible pace, raising high expectations for its future. As you look ahead to the next one or two years, what are some key white spaces you've identified for Zepto's growth?

One type of growth is very traditional—launch more dark stores, expand to more neighborhoods, more cities, more countries. The second type of growth is actually a lot cooler, which is category expansion. So Zepto Café, makeup essentials, going deep into meat as a category; at some point, pharmacy, and alcohol in the states where alcohol is allowed, and all these other categories. Quick e-commerce today is at a very nascent stage. Last monsoon in Mumbai and Bengaluru, we were selling umbrellas. It was a hit. It has nothing to do with groceries, but it's what people needed.

Many people think that what we built is a grocery business. I beg to differ! What we built is a super-efficient logistics and delivery network. Now, it's just a question of working backward from the customer's basket, asking them what they need, and providing them with that. It's essential to get into more categories and more use cases and be able to capture more wallet share from customers. We essentially need to know how to make an existing customer spend more.

How did you ensure the quality of services?

We had no experience doing this, so we hired someone excellent from a competitor company, someone who had done it before, to now build it for us. He had learnt a lot from the learning curves.

Did you encounter any issues with the initial hiring of delivery partners?

Initially, no, because when we were launching our first dark store, we just needed ten partners. That was easy as we hired one, and he knew ten others who came on board. But then we went through this phase in 2021 when we launched three or four dark stores in August. In the next couple of months—from 1 September to 31 December—we went from five to seventy-seven stores across cities. That phase was a challenge, but it was fixed over time. A while later, the industry as a whole faced a shortage as a large number of delivery partners had gone back home for a month or two. That posed a challenge for us. Now, it's easier because if we open two stores in a particular neighbourhood, we can divide the capacity and offer shorter distances and travel times, which makes the entire process faster for both consumers and us. We have riders with cycles and e-bikes who can't cover the distance of one or two kilometres but can cover under one kilometre, and that penetration of vehicles proves to be a great contribution.

Was there a training programme offered to the delivery partners in the beginning, and how did you manage the overall economics of it?

Unlike a food marketplace, wherein a delivery partner could be going all across the city in one day, our model is that our delivery partners originate from a central place, which are our dark stores. When the delivery is done, they come back to it. That lets us have a lot more control over their training and onboarding process. Before they do their first delivery, they go through a one or two-day delivery training programme. It includes training them on how to use the app and the principles of road safety.

We also partnered with a lot of local police stations. We'd get officers from the stations to come in and do training on road safety.

We are now starting to work on the learning and development aspect, which is how we can get some more delivery partners to escalate their careers much faster. For instance, if you're a delivery partner, how can we get you to a place where you're managing a fleet of delivery partners, eventually to keep growing through the organization?

Did you use a hybrid payment structure for the delivery partners?

A layman assumes that the delivery partner chooses to work for a company based on how much they get paid in return. That's not the case. What actually matters is how easy you make their life.

Our model is to limit the partners' delivery area to around a kilometre and a half since that ensures the delivery partners get proper space to sit, use charging stations, and washrooms. We provide them with snacks, food, and water at different times of the day.

These things, which are perhaps basic to us as consumers, are critical to a delivery partner. As a result of all of this, our rider retention is considerably higher than that of a food delivery marketplace.

How do you navigate the market when your customer experience is solely dependent on someone who is not on your payroll?

It is in our best interest that our delivery partners are safe and that they behave really well.

The reason we've been able to do a pretty good job of it so far is because all of these partners start at a centralized place, which is not the case for other delivery brands or cab service companies that are absolutely decentralized.

These delivery partners visit the store about twenty times a day, so they are able to internalize the behaviour we want to influence, and that gives us a lot of control over how we operate. Eventually, that control helps us in ensuring they are wearing the Zepto T-shirts and riding safely.

Customers are still being influenced by market rates, so where do you see the next differentiation point coming?

That question has a couple of generalizations that I slightly disagree with. For one, the idea that the faster you grow, the more expensive products become is one misconception.

The truth is, the faster we deliver, the cheaper it becomes for us. There are a couple of aspects to it: Speed—can we assure this is the fastest you're going to get your delivery and create trust on it; assortment and availability—if a consumer needs a particular thing, despite the long time it takes, they want it or else it's no show; pricing—delivery fees and the pricing of the product, the idea is not to be the cheapest available alternative but at the same time, one shouldn't feel they are getting ripped off; quality—how fresh the fruits and vegetables are, which is critical to the consumers.

We need to be consistently strong and winning in all the four aspects at the same time, and that entrenches us from the competition. That circles back to my initial point of execution—we should be able to execute all of these consistently.

Dev Arora

Dev Arora has a true strategic mindset and comes with over two decades' worth of experience across sales, distribution, operations, and other critical segments of FMCG businesses. He is the former CEO of Chai Point's CPG vertical and has transformed the tea category in India by disrupting the traditional market space.

His innovative decisions around packaging and growing the business in such a way that eases the lives of true chai connoisseurs is beyond excellence. Before Chai Point, he played an integral part at Hindustan Coca Cola Limited and the ITC group.

CHAPTER 9

The Many Faces and Emotions of Chai

In conversation with Dev Arora, Former CEO of Chai Point

India is obsessed with its beverages, especially tea, and in this conversation, Dev Arora points out how serving personalized tea options offered Chai Point an edge in this extensive beverage-consuming nation. He takes us through the psyche of a consumer and what brands like Chai Point can offer beyond a cup of chai. Dev goes on to explain how it is about an affordable experience and how he looks at those in the same industry as enablers, not competitors. As a leader, Dev discusses the key insights from a business standpoint and their revenue-generating models.

* * *

In India, evenings are the time when Indians typically take a chai break, so it's great we are having this conversation at chai time.

Adding my bit to it: Chai is time-, occasion-, and age-agnostic, and this opinion has been built over the data I have observed, not because of my bias towards the business I am leading. Data says that tea consumption from 3.30 p.m. to 5 p.m. (which is an ideal time for chai consumption in India) is the same as how much consumption takes place between 1 p.m. and 3 p.m. I firmly believe that every time is tea time.

> *Chai is time-, occasion-, and age-agnostic.*

At the moment, in January 2024, what are some exciting things happening at Chai Point?

A lot, in fact. We are the core believers of 'staying true to one's category', and that leads to the question we ask ourselves: 'How can we expand the category?'

Many businesses around would try to lead the category or would try to contain the category to themselves. But that has not been our philosophy because the category of chai is huge. Even fifty Chai Points in India can't do justice to the category. Eventually, we stabilized ourselves and looked for avenues wherein we could go and serve the story.

In our case, we started with retail, then moved ahead to bigger corporations. While exploring different avenues, we saw a gap in the market—the experience that people were having after consuming tea that was delivered to them was bad. That led to the innovation of the flask in which the tea gets delivered in India now. Having innovated it ourselves, we had all the opportunity to patent it and keep it to ourselves. Soon, the realization hit us that when others would want to explore this category further, they would use a substandard material, which would lead to a bad experience for the consumer. That can lead to people believing the core myth that *'chai jaa ke peena acha hai, delivery mein nahi.'* Chai tastes better when you go to a spot and have it, not when it's delivered. Thus, the innovation of the flask was opened for use to the public, and we decided to let everyone deliver using it.

It would cause us some market share loss, but eventually, the category would grow, and looking at retail, now we get about 50% of our revenue just through delivery. Contrary to popular belief, these are not just office deliveries, but even deliveries at homes. The hook for such a response is that you stay true to your category and don't try to contain it, but rather expand on it. That's the core job of a leader—

ensuring that the category expands, and only then will the business keep expanding. Otherwise, what's the fun of being a leader in a 100-crore category? Be a leader in a 1,00,000 crore category, and chai is already one such category.

> *The way to get a great response from consumers is by staying true to your category, not trying to contain it; rather, try to expand it, even at the cost of some losses.*

Later, we saw an opportunity in offices and workplaces where people are struggling to get satisfaction through the right beverage. There are dip teas, coffees, and premixes of beverages, but the craving for chai is a different feeling altogether. We tapped on it—put multiple heat-resistant decanters that would keep the beverage hot and installed them in offices during longer periods of the day.

Circling back on tea being time-agnostic, we noticed that people would consume it as and when they wished, not waiting for a particular time frame to indulge. Some of these places we served came back to us and asked, 'Why don't you put a permanent setup here?' It was a great idea. We did that, but being a tech-first founding team, we realized that we must scale our model. To do that, we started investing in developing a bot that can deliver chai, and more essentially *Ghar jaisi chai*, tea that tastes home-made.

We tested that model in India, and it did well, but it was tough to scale after, looking at the size and complexities the machine came with. We took another chance, went abroad, met manufacturing partners, and got some more options to satiate our craving of building a model that always gives fresh chai off a cup. 'Up and Coming' is the same model by us, a bot that would prepare chai by the cup. Similar to a coffee machine that brews a hot cup in thirty seconds, we have now developed a machine that makes chai like that. You get hot water, tea leaves, milk, and sugar; and you get brewed chai in less than a minute. Icing on the cake: It's fully developed and manufactured in

India. Another exciting feature this machine will soon have is a touch of personalization: Whether you want milk at a 70% level or 40%, you will be able to customize your beverage.

At Chai Point, how many cups do you sell a day?

We serve more than a million cups a day, but that's still a very small number. The consumption of chai out of the home is more than 500 million a day. From bustling railway stations to crowded hospitals, bus stands, courtrooms, and offices—chai is everywhere.

What does the future look like for Chai Point, considering the competition?

We are looking at 'everyone' as someone who's enhancing this category and giving a better experience to chai. To put things in perspective, India is a tea-drinking nation through and through. But the question we get asked all the time is, 'Why chai? Coffee has always been a premium beverage, and it would have been easy to sell coffee. Who would pay as much for a chai as people pay for their coffee?' But the point of discussion is, 'Doesn't a consumer need that?' Before Domino's entered the market, it was Nirula's that brought the concept of eating pizza to most of us. One would have wondered why people would want pizza here. But they did create a category that never existed before. Now, for many of us, chai is a part of our cultural fabric, and till a while ago, one did not have a nice place to have chai. People used to crave a good cup of this beverage in the best hotels of the country. This opportunity is huge, it can accommodate a lot of players and generate employment.

Talking about competition, we are not running to grab market share from the competitors. We are working towards trying to get a good product to the person who's already out and wants the product. Can we do it all by ourselves? No. Can we do it faster? The answer is still no, but we'll be able to do it better and faster only when other players are setting up the ground.

We are there to provide good chai with consistency in it to the consumer who is going out and consuming it. Eventually, we will need more enablers. We need more people working on this beverage, making the consumer ready to come sit, chat, pay the right amount, and get a great experience while elevating the market. You can now find our bots in some properties owned by ITC and Taj Groups, and simultaneously, we are also enabling the small tea sellers by developing bots for them, which will have that particular chaiwallah's recipe. It's undeniably true that all cities have that one chaiwallah that people love to visit. These bots will increase their productivity—sellers can prepare easy-to-take snacks that go with chai; they don't have to make chai again and again, and so on. All this will elevate the income of the vendor. That's why we don't see others who are selling chai as competition. We see them as enablers and enhancers.

Those who are selling chai, we don't see them as competitors but as enablers and enhancers.

What is this bot like?

It's a sleek machine that can be put in smaller spaces and runs on the proprietary software that we own. Everything is stored on the cloud, so it can have more than a billion recipes on it. One great feature, as aforementioned and yet to launch, is how this machine will enhance accessibility for consumers. If one person likes chai a particular way, they can easily follow their routine in the office as well. They will simply have to scan a QR code in a store, and the machine will automatically recognize the consumer and their preference for a specific kind of chai.

What is the leading and highest revenue generator business model for you?

All our businesses, though related, are different in nature. The first segment is our retail business; second and third are vending machines, and alongside that is a D2C (Direct to Consumer) model, both of which come under the overall CPG (Consumer Packaged Goods) portfolio we maintain; then there is a SaaS (Software as a Service) arm that makes billing solutions for some leading eateries easier. We call our retail business our 'brand vector' because that introduces our customer to us and vice versa. Chances are that you know about Chai Point because you have seen an outlet somewhere. It's not a mere coincidence, and this is what we call a brand vector. This visibility contributes to almost 50% of our revenue. Then, the CPG arm—consisting of the vending machine business and the other D2C segment—contributes the remaining 50%. SaaS is very small as of now, so its contribution is negligible. The business that we are really pushing through is our vending business. It is seven years younger than the retail business and was significantly impacted by COVID because offices were closed; however, despite that, the business is now growing and coming closer to being as big as our retail business.

What drove you to scale this business at such a rapid pace? From a business growth perspective, what are some key insights you've gained along the way?

One thing that I believe we have been good at is actively listening to our customers. We are a Bengaluru-based company, and when we were serving our product around, we saw a great demand from around the neighbourhood, as a lot of cups were getting delivered to offices every single day. That gave rise to the innovation of the 'flask' that you see chai getting delivered in. Later, we started getting bulk orders for chai, and that led to the thought of, 'Why not create a bot that makes chai, which is available 24/7, free of human interference, and is consistent each time?' Soon we realized with growth, that rarely people consume their chai without any spices—ginger, cardamom, masala—so we introduced those flavours; in addition to flavours like lemongrass for the West Coast, Irani for Hyderabad, fennel seeds and carom seeds for those who like their chai that way post-lunch.

We learnt a few things while we were listening to our customers. One, we cannot scale up really fast at the price point we operate on at our stores. We would need a much affordable and lucrative price point. There are two ways of approaching it: Rent a store or install a bot. Keeping things cost-effective, a bot in today's time, especially in places like airports, is a much better idea. That's why we think this is the brand vector that can scale the business, not only in offices but even in railway stations. That's what we are working towards—building brand identities for tea vendors, creating a whole ecosystem, and letting the consumers make an impression for themselves with a good cup to hold when they are boarding their trains. For tea vendors, this would simultaneously increase their productivity and enhance consistency.

Quick Sips: Rapid Q&A with Dev Arora:

1. **Describe yourself in three words**

   Energy, Extrovert, Tea Lover.

   A short story behind being a tea lover—not related to me being the CEO of Chai Point—is when I was working from home during the COVID days, my daughter reminded me of my over-consumption of tea in many forms. From green to milk-based, to black tea to others. It led me to consciously restrict my consumption, but it was to a point where I was having fourteen-odd cups a day.

2. **If you were not doing what you're doing, what else would be your profession?**

   I would have started something of my own.

3. **If your life were a movie, what movie or what genre would that be?**

   Certainly, comedy as a genre; I enjoy innocent comedies like *Andaaz Apna Apna,* so probably that one.

4. **Every leader experiences moments of loneliness at the top. What is one source of inspiration that keeps you motivated and grounded?**

   I turn to the people I work with every day. There is a solid reason behind it. I finished high school, finished a course through a distance learning program, and started working. My first job was to sell credit cards through cold calling; then I moved to the FMCG sector and worked there till I finished graduation. Since then, I have been worshipping humans because there's always so much to learn. After graduating, I worked at ITC, and after working for about twenty-one years now, I still find those working around me very inspiring. I worship them and learn from them. I believe that I will not be able to talk with those revolutionary figures who passed on decades ago, so it's better to watch and learn from those around you and seek inspiration.

5. **Your favourite superhero.**

   I'd say Captain America, only because my kid has made me watch so much of it.

6. **Your favourite song.**

   Not a song, maybe, but one poem that is one of my favourites is *Koshish Karne Waalon Ki Kabhi Haar Nahi Hoti*.

7. **What is the next thing in tech that you would bet your money on?**

   I would bet my money on platforms with strong technologies that help brands unique to different parts of the country prosper. Take the Kanwal brand for example, it's a very famous brand in Kashmir but we don't see it around in metro cities; despite its interesting range. One must get an opportunity to explore these products and brands and eventually these should be made available. Consumption would become more buoyant with more options, and these brands should get that opportunity.

8. **What is your favourite brand?**

   Chai Point. What can be more important and favourite than the brand you are building?

9. **Then the second favourite brand, in this case. Or the most iconic brand in your view.**

   It would be Haldiram's. I am inspired by how they have navigated distribution. I have a very close affinity for the regional brands, and I want to see them growing.

Dilsher Malhi

Dilsher Malhi is the founder and CEO of Zupee, a skill-based gaming company, a game that drives around human pyschology and behaviour. He was featured among the young tech entrepreneurs in the esteemed list of 'Forbes 30 under 30 Asia', 2021. An alumnus of IIT Kanpur, Dilsher's deep interests lie in understanding human behaviour and its various psychological concepts. His journey reflects a mix of bold decisions, a willingness to embrace failure, and a sharp understanding of business fundamentals in the gaming space.

CHAPTER 10

Gamer to Game Changer: The All-Out Approach to Gaming in India

In conversation with Dilsher Malhi, Founder and CEO of Zupee

In this candid exploration of the human psyche, Dilsher Malhi takes the reader on a ride through mindsets and strategies that a founder builds to navigate the complexities of the gaming industry and startup life. From discussing the balance between innovation at each new step and market realities to understanding the importance of human psychology in game mechanics, Dilsher shares insights on growing a business, retaining talent, and the evolution of his entrepreneurial journey from day one to today.

The conversation also touches on handling investments, decision-making processes, and how the post-pandemic landscape reshaped engagement for the gaming industry. This conversation explores the concepts of leadership, business growth, and the challenges of scaling in a rapidly evolving industry.

❖❖❖

Looking back at your early days, even those in Bikaner, were there any moments or experiences that made you realize you were cut out for entrepreneurship?

I hailed from Rajasthan, and my father, who is now retired, had a government job in the Police department, which comes with its own set of transfers every couple of years. Coming from a lower-middle class background, the concept of pocket money seldom existed. However, I always had an itch to hack monetization. I did many interesting things back in those days, which I am not necessarily proud of, but let me share one for context. I had organized a pen fighting tournament and had prepared everything that was required—a round robin structure, an inner purchases model to buy complex pens where one goes inside the other—and I was famous for organizing such games across the school. My seniors would call me to carry out such events, and I believe I got too famous, as one time, the principal called me in and wrote a diary note which was a double jeopardy—you get scolded by the principal and then you have to tell your parents about the diary note leading to more scolding. Eventually, my pens were confiscated, but ultimately, we were net profitable, so that was a good thing.

In essence, my upbringing, coupled with my fascination around hacking monetization, led me to this. Now that I look back, another factor was that as a teenager, one tries to bridge the financial gap. The gap that comes in when they see those of the same age around them being slightly more well off than themselves. Taking matters into my own hands gave me a slight flavour of entrepreneurship.

Another such instance was how I'd lose in both indoor games and outdoor sports while playing with my brother, who is eight years older than me. Constantly losing instilled competitiveness in me, and in my defense, after clearing fifth or sixth grade, I never lost when I played against him. That's another way characters are shaped while growing up.

Then came the time to pick the stream after I cleared JEE. I entered IIT Kanpur and studied civil engineering. Little did I know that one rarely gets a good package through this stream. All the hard work, studies, and dreams of a great monetary package led to this unfortunate realization. Following everyone else who didn't bag a computer science stream, I, too, started the process of changing streams. I moved to chemical engineering, and that's when the journey got interesting for me. It was mandatory to take a course from the humanities, so I went ahead and pursued Introduction to Psychology, which was a game changer. There was no specific coursework, and the material was extensive, so I had to read a lot. I started by studying evolutionary biology—how we develop from one cell to multicellular organisms; anthropology—how cultures shaped us; then came genetics, parent–child relationships, hormones, neurotransmitters, neuroscience, etc. These aspects allow for a slight peek inside the human mind, and all our behaviours are shared by these processes. Interestingly, when everyone else was getting into robotics clubs, I was focusing on humanities.

Soon, it was time for each student to intern. I joined a company as an intern and disliked their way of working. I then decided I would not work for a corporate setup and had broadly generalized the entire industry based on my experience. I was then left with two options: Research and entrepreneurship. I considered pursuing research in bio-medics because of evolutionary biology. Microfluidics is the domain wherein you can marry the logic of chemical engineering with biology. I went to Switzerland (I had a very romanticized version of going abroad!) and did a good job while interning, but soon it struck me that this is not what I want to pursue, since in bio-medics, one can never be sure when the impact will really come into play.

Eventually, there came a point when all options were eliminated, and I was left to execute something of my own. I have a broader thesis around how I look at businesses. One framework that stood out for me was from the book *Hooked* by Nir Eyal. It states that there are 'vitamins' and 'painkillers', which the author has used as metaphors to talk about various products. Painkillers solve problems, just like all businesses around us do—Ola, Uber, Zomato; and then there are vitamins, which don't make your problems go away but simply enhance the quality of life—Facebook, Snapchat, gaming apps, etc. The reason this framework resonated with me was that I understood that I need to live my life, not just follow the standard process of waking up, eating, and sleeping. Vitamins, as metaphors to enhancing the quality of life, are equally important to have. And since vitamins are designed around fundamental human motivations, it was clear to me that I'd make a vitamin. That's how the thesis started coming together.

The fundamental motivation of any cell or species is reproduction, as opposed to survival. Essentially, that translates to one making copies of themselves before they die. Now, these fundamental motivations manifest in everything we do. Species make decisions by observing small biomarkers; so ideally, if there is a plethora of information being shared, one would focus only on a few of those details which evolution has hardwired us for with time. Take female lions for example; they are only attracted to male lions who have intense beards, which depicts survival surplus. In the extreme hot weather of Africa, if a lion can maintain their body temperature with that heavy beard, it signifies their absolute confidence.

> *Species make decisions by observing small biomarkers; so ideally, if there is a plethora of information being shared, one would focus only on a few of those details that evolution has hardwired for us with time.*

Subconsciously, the idea is to focus on smaller bits to make decisions. Look for very small things and make decisions. Humans and conglomerates also function in similar ways. Coca-Cola as a brand has hit a significant mark because we are hardwired to get dopamine hits once we consume beverages high in carbs and fats. Our ancestors were hardwired to consume diets high in carbs and fats because they'd be predated by animals, and that was one hook these companies found. So, corn and sugar production went through the roof. Another example is that we are hardwired to focus on 'us versus them' theories, so we fight for football clubs, religions, and politics. Six-pack abs signal aerobics agility, and that's why many of us get attracted to these abs, which in turn leads to survival surplus. Indian weddings are another example of such a phenomenon. We save for decades to spend on a two-day affair since that highlights status-seeking behaviour. Why is status-seeking behaviour yet another phenomenon of fundamental motivations for humans? Because the higher both parties are in the status hierarchy, better mating partners will be available, thus leading to better progeny patterns. That's why we engage in games of status; we might not consciously know why we are doing this, but essentially, this is how we are hardwired.

Similarly, to understand anthropology, one great example is to understand the significance jewellry has. Long ago, tribal leaders or kings were the only ones who could wear rare gems and stones. These stones have a higher status associated with them, and similarly, many housing apartments in cities like Gurugram have British or American names, owing to colonization, and these names represent higher social status. Ideally, the world is run by people who understand this machinery really well. If you can understand this machinery, you can design anything, create anything, and build anything.

This is a fascinating understanding of human behaviour. Can you take us through your journey of discovering what you wanted to focus on and develop?

Struggle is quite romanticized in our culture, and that is something I refrain from discussing. Many believe that execution is supremely important to disrupt the surroundings. While that is partially true, ideas that take place before execution are equally supreme. Take Facebook, for example, which came out of thin air. It was all about the idea first, and similarly, we at Zupee like to play in dead space. We wanted to understand what humans really want. And that's when we came up with this thesis that, in the end, humans are a pleasure-seeking species. Parallelly, I was studying culture and came across Nietzsche's famous statement, 'God is dead', and thought, 'What does that even mean?' That meant a movement from a religious thought to a scientific one wherein people realized there is no afterlife and that earthly happiness is the only supreme happiness.

Two myths rule our lives: Romanticism and consumerism. Romanticism is accepting that human feelings are the biggest authority. Earlier, killing someone was bad because it was written so in our religious texts, and now it is bad because it causes suffering. Consumerism says that if you're feeling bad, it's your fault and that you're not experiencing, consuming, or travelling enough. If you do, then that exceptional moment will kick in, and your life will get better. What that translates to is that as a society, our craving for pleasant sensations is at an all-time high, and our tolerance for unpleasant sensations is at an all-time low. We tapped into this and realized that is what humans really want.

The form factor today is gaming for us; ten years out, we might be doing something extremely different than what we are doing today. So, we focused our minds on what it is we can design that creates the most pleasurable experience for people. We started thinking and came across the idea of flow state, which means that you are so engrossed in a particular moment that the moment absorbs you. Many learned intellectuals like Plato, Aristotle, and Socrates have talked about the concept of flow state. It is one concept that is pervasive across genders, age, culture, etc., and this fascination piqued our curiosity further. We asked ourselves, can we design those flow experiences? The best form factor today is games. In the gaming setups, if we play something very easy, boredom kicks in; if it is very difficult, anxiety hits. So the crux is to design something keeping that balance in mind. Gaming designers do that really well—precisely increasing the skills to match the demand of the player. That's precisely how flow state is achieved.

But there are three conditions to that. One is that skills and demands should meet; second is that there must be direct feedback; and third is that failure should matter. An example of this is rock climbing. It's a dangerous activity, yet many do it. The reason is because they are in a flow state—a state wherein they see the next rock to climb as a pattern and keep climbing till they reach the top. This proved to be very powerful. Now the real question was, can we make this a tool to further elevate education, trauma resolution, physical well-being, and even elevate human subconsciousness? That is the vision we have. Certainly, it's huge, and we can't transform education in one day, but the most proven format of flow state comes in gaming.

We can go deeper into gaming and the business I am building. Building it involves monetization, which is a critical aspect, and our model is pay-to-play as opposed to free-to-play. In traditional gaming, monetization happens through advertisements and in-app purchases, and unfortunately, that doesn't work in India. The reason being, it directly questions the worth of your attention. In such a low GDP-per-capita country with such a population, why should your attention be worth more? That's exactly what is reflected in our advertisement rates. Revenue-per-download in India is 1/200 of what it is in the U.S. At one point, India accounted for 33% of PUBG's global downloads and less than 1% of revenue. That's how skewed the numbers are.

We then started putting the ideas together on how to design and involve failure in the game—since it matters in the flow state—and make it work. Rock climbing is exactly that. One is so engrossed in it because they know if their foot slips, they'll fall. So how could we bring that small skin in the game wherein a small amount of risk leads to a small amount of reward? In the real money gaming space, there are three major segments. One is daily fantasy sports, which is owned by Dream11, which is now approximately $8 billion; second is the cards gaming space, which includes poker and rummy. There are about 500 million gamers, and about 150 million to 200 million of which are involved in fantasy while 40 million or 50 million are involved in card gaming. There was a third space called casual games where there were no big players, so we decided to jump in. In this segment, we take popular concepts and tweak the mechanics of the game in such a way that the final engagement and monetization are far superior to the traditional games. We are often called a gaming platform, but that is something I don't prefer myself. I'd rather be called a neuroscience platform. Currently, we are just at Version 1 of it.

> *Everyone has a different risk appetite and backgrounds they come from, so then often it becomes a question of 'when'. When to take that risk and when to jump into something, rather than a question that demands a simple yes or no.*

Penetrating the startup world is a challenge. How can one decide between letting go of the security of a job and starting something of their own or saving up to sustain themselves and then starting something of their own?

The answer to this can be quite subjective, and one direction I believe in is the 'debug mode'. Why do I have certain desires, how deep are they, and why do I want to become a founder? There is a famous story 'Pot of Gold'—so one who loves to dig, will keep digging here and there not worrying about the outcome until he eventually finds the gold; but the one who is only determined to find the pot of gold might not, since he will just stop digging after a few feet into the ground. The real question we should be asking ourselves is why we want to do a particular thing, how deep is that desire, and why is it the right thing to do in the first place? The true answer comes after asking these questions to ourselves.

Everyone has a different risk appetite and background they come from, so often it becomes a question of 'when'. When to take that risk and when to jump into something, rather than a question that demands a simple yes or no.

What do you think about this wide obsession over 'Product-Market Fit' (PMF)? At Zupee, what was that journey of achieving PMF, and where do you think you are on that journey right now?

Someone once mentioned that PMF should be called Market-Product Fit. The bigger truth is always the market, and, of course, one can create a market for a product, but the market is the ultimate truth. This brings me back to the fact that if you have a good thesis around something, only then do you start iterating around it. After designing many games that didn't work, we would go back to the iterations we made and the feedback we sought. Those aspects would help us analyze why a particular factor worked well but the other didn't. The real answer is 'data': The metric of growth is how many non-incentivized customers are transacting on your platform every month. That is the real growth and PMF. Even at Zupee, it has been a journey, and it's a playbook that keeps evolving.

As someone who is ahead in their startup journey with data points to look back on, what is your advice to those who are sitting in classrooms with their paper plans? How much validation should they seek as a starter, and how many people do they experiment with? Especially to build that conviction that they are headed in the right direction.

First, it is important to notice and identify a behaviour pattern and see if there is a way to optimize it. For example, cabs have been around for a while, but they weren't always reliable. But now, how interesting is the idea that regardless of the weather, a cab is coming all the way to pick you up. My concern with today's education system is that schools must teach human behaviour and human motivation since our teammates, investors, and users are all human. The common saying that goes like 'India is full of great engineers who know the "what" and "how" of it, but not the "why" of it', is true.

What is your advice on when to start fundraising, and should one start with being bootstrapped or should one seek fundraising purely on the idea?

There is a common saying that goes, 'Business is the rocket, and funding is the fuel. ' I'd say get into the fundraising aspect early because it's not easy and is quite a long process that is filled with rejections. That's why I insist on having a strong 'why' that helps build a business.

Coming back to the question, it's important to understand why you want to do something and have a good understanding of it. You need to believe that it's worth the time and effort and ask yourself if this is something you see yourself doing for a long time. It's very easy to think that we'll build a business and exit in two years, but in real life, it doesn't work that way. MakeMyTrip was listed in the early 2000s, and they are still running it. It should not be seen as an easy way out.

I can share my experience and framework on how to go about raising funds. It's a multivariate analysis, but I will share the top five to six variables I look at. First, can we lead the fund since someone has to price it? Second, what is their relevant experience in this industry or sector? Third, their reputation and past data. For example, how have they been with the founders? Fourth, is to understand valuation sensitivity—each fund has a different valuation sensitivity. Fifth, how fast can they move, i.e., start funding? And sixth is to understand if they can put in the following capital. It is amazing to have someone on the cap table who can deploy such huge funds consistently that they don't need to raise capital again. Another important metric is to understand the percentage of funds that are already deployed. For example, if someone says they have 2 billion Assets Under Management (AUM), but 90% of them are deployed, then it's of no use to us.

Given the examples of investment mistakes that founders make, how does someone decide whether they should go ahead with a certain investment or not?

When making an investment decision, always stay grounded in first principles. Understand your reasons for pursuing it—are they 'nice-to-have' or 'must-have'? Consider both positive and negative potential consequences. For instance, when I raised my seed round, someone advised me that running out of money is the biggest risk. So, you need a solid 'why' and a backup plan. It's a nuanced decision, and context plays a big role, but having a clear rationale is crucial.

How did you go about collecting all this information?

The idea is to go to people who have done things far better than you and ask them questions because they have the answers. To me, there is intellectual understanding, and then there is visceral understanding. It helps to know if a certain person has been there and done that. And other than that, the DNA of being shamelessly curious. You keep asking, and you keep researching, and that's it.

Your ideas drive home the point that you don't need to reinvent the wheel. Instead, find people who are ahead of you in that journey so that you can learn from them and then catch up.

Newton once said, 'If I have seen further, it is by standing on the shoulders of giants.' That's precisely the point: Go to people who have done that. In my experience, most of them are willing to help. If they see a genuine desire, even before you have equity, people agree to help.

Why do you think many founders today are not able to strike that balance between growth and profitability?

It depends on how solid the thesis is. In India, the thesis needs to be nuanced for all the tier-1, -2, and -3 cities since they behave differently. To sell utility and monetize in tier-2 and tier-3 cities is very difficult, especially if you are interested in making it a business with high margins. There are two major reasons for that. One, there is no money—90% of Indians earn between $1,700 to $2,000 a year.

Second, any country wherein people missed the Industrial Revolution and weren't trained to pay on an hourly basis didn't truly value their own time. Saying, give me money, and I will save your time, doesn't actually work.

Thirdly, let's understand the VC ecosystem. They would show that the markup is done and will also want to show a higher IRR (Investment Return Rate) for the next fundraise. There is a saying that goes, startups are sitting on the lion, thinking that it reflects growth, but the moment they step down, the lion will eat them alive. That is where I believe startups go wrong—the PMF isn't defined, sharp clarity doesn't exist, VC's money is already in, founders are young (not that I am a fifty-year-old founder), but they want it all very fast. Fundamentally, if your business is rock solid, then the growth and profitability will grow in a similar direction. Of course, there are other nuances to consider, like if Ola and Uber don't have enough drivers and cars are still taking twenty-five minutes to reach, then no one would consider booking through those apps. I met around eight to ten gaming founders at ChinaJoy, the biggest gaming event in China, and I asked the founders there how much funds they had raised. They replied, none, because this is a cloud business, and if in such a business you are losing money, then there is a cause for concern. Ultimately, a business has to make money. If you are sacrificing on that—unless you have a strategic reason like to capture the market or defensibility—be very careful with why you are doing that.

How have you evolved in the past five years as a founder?

I don't have a favourite team, only favourite players—like Kevin De Bruyne at Manchester City or Steph Curry at the Golden State Warriors. However, I have learned to move beyond the romanticized idea of being a lone wolf. The leader, army, and the culture—all should be amazing. Everyone says that core values are important, but only after you hit that point of failure do you realize how crucial those values are for building a successful startup.

The biggest evolution for me has been recognizing that it's not just about intellect or skill but also about aligning with the right people, sharing values, and growing together. As a founder, you experience a lot of self-doubt, especially when you're starting. You will question if you're good enough. But through the trials, you develop a deeper sense of peace and self-confidence. It's a fast-tracked maturity, almost like commando training, where you're constantly forced to step up.

> *The biggest evolution for me has been recognizing that it's not just about intellect or skill but also about aligning with the right people, sharing values, and growing together.*

In the startup world, there's no hiding. It's a place where your blind spots are exposed, and that's a great thing if you're committed to growth. I truly believe entrepreneurs drive civilization forward—look at inventors who changed the world with fire, electricity, or the internet. I have immense respect for entrepreneurs and believe they are essential for progress. If you look at explorers of old, they would pitch themselves to their kings to allow them to have materials and ships, and in exchange, they would fetch gold for them or expand their territory. Those were the real startup founders. If we had fifty to sixty driven entrepreneurs in India, we could change the entire country. Entrepreneurs don't just build businesses, they create jobs, pay taxes, and contribute to the ecosystem. It's a non-zero-sum game—everyone benefits.

How have the government intervention policies impacted Zupee's journey, and how do you, as founders, influence policies in the gaming industry's favour?

It's a global fact that policies follow tech because tech is done by individuals who don't need consensus and can move fast. Firstly, policy, laws, or states are run on consensus. It's clear that games of skill are okay in a pay-to-play model, but games of chance are not okay. Secondly, the bigger point is awareness and education—who you are, what you are, and why you are as a company. How does one identify the clear line between the game of skill and the game of chance? To identify that, we have designed a data-driven framework because games of skill are driven by data and based on mathematical or scientific facts. This framework defines for us what a game of skill and what a game of chance is. Thirdly, one needs to understand the concerns. Concerns help users protect their interests, and you, as a founder, need to be very responsible. It's your moral and ethical responsibility and, in essence, is just good business sense.

Earlier, each state could ban gaming, but now it's all centralized, which is better. Gaming is the pinnacle of entertainment and is truly even bigger than that. It's interactive entertainment, unlike movies or songs, which you passively consume. That is reflected in both qualitative and quantitative figures. Now, we are in the digital ecosystem, wherein our fundamental needs include engaging and having people around us. Essentially, it boils down to how you can build a thriving ecosystem and have responsible and safe checks in place.

What checks do you have in place to control issues like addiction?

Every platform has to be morally and ethically responsible. It's such a fine balance. If there is no dopamine hit, no one will open that app. Retention, in essence, is a dopamine hit. Sustainable businesses are only those that play smartly. Take Netflix as an example. People always ask if Netflix will produce a series that is so interesting that we'll feel like watching another episode. The answer is, of course, they will. That's their business.

You once mentioned that you focus on raw and young talent as opposed to those with industry experience of over three years. Why is that?

We are open to hiring everyone, not just freshers. Our approach is different from many companies. We consider ourselves one of the most innovative companies, and we're constantly working towards staying that way. For us, it's about unlearning and relearning. Here's an example: When we're kids, we're taught to respect our elders, and whenever we ask questions, we're often silenced with fear. Then, at twenty-five, we're expected to suddenly overcome that fear. But it doesn't work that way. We, at Zupee, focus on cultivating the right habits, investing in people, and unlocking their full potential. We prefer fresh perspectives, but it's not about age. What matters is where you are and, most importantly, where you want to be. If someone has that inner drive, that hunger to transcend and reach their highest potential, they'll get there no matter how long it takes. They don't need an external push.

If one wants to be a product manager at your company, what skills would you recommend?

There is no checklist, if you have the raw materials that I spoke about, then you are good to go. That is the way we operate. There is no checklist. We are creating for the future and looking for the DNA that can help us do that. It's not about getting a certain four skills that one can easily acquire. But the answer is desire.

When we discuss ideas with others, there is always a lingering fear or doubt that someone will copy and implement it. How do we deal with that uncertainty?

When starting, I too, went through that phase of wondering if I should share my ideas out loud because I thought someone would steal them. But I've learned that founders are deeply connected to their companies, like a parent is to their child. Others can't replicate that love and passion. While someone can copy, it's a low probability in my experience.

As for defensibility, it's not about making your idea impossible to disrupt—everything is disruptable. It's about finding what makes certain businesses resilient. Take WhatsApp, for example. When they updated their terms, everyone was ready to jump to Signal or Telegram. But who actually left? Hardly anyone. You can research companies that are hard to disrupt and analyze why. Look at why startups often beat big companies: They're nimble, and they move fast. Big corporations, on the other hand, are stuck down with layers of approval. So, while disruption is always possible, it's about the risk appetite, adaptability, and understanding patterns. When you do that, you'll see which areas are more defensible and which aren't.

What are the things that companies focus on to increase the LTV (Lifetime Value) of the user? Is there a marketing strategy where you can maintain a CAC (Customer Acquisition Cost) while acquiring these users?

Any good business optimizes for both. A strong LTV means little if your CAC is too high, so striking a balance is key. For us, marketing and advertising are often confused, but they are distinct: Marketing is about understanding human motivations, while advertising is the tool to convey that. A solid product with great word of mouth often takes care of the marketing side.

Our approach to user acquisition is simple: Understand who your users are, what you need to tell them, and when and where to reach them. There's a 'magic number' for how many times you need to engage a user before converting them—after that, additional impressions are wasted. Once you've identified the right user and message, it's all about finding the most cost-effective places to show them that message, whether digitally or physically. With the right strategy, you can acquire high-value users with minimal spending.

How did you manage to retain the human psychology aspect within the app or different use cases?

Human psychology isn't a Band-Aid that you can press on your skin. It's a framework that seeps deep. It starts with understanding who the users are, why they're using the app, and what they need to hear. Every element of the app, from messaging to channels, is designed with this in mind.

For example, think of how Disney consistently creates blockbusters. They understand the neuroscience behind storytelling—how to craft a hero, a villain, and a redemption arc. Similarly, when designing game mechanics, we tap into these principles. While players might not always realize it, everything from traditional game dynamics to our own app features is built with human psychology at its core.

We are essentially incorporating models from the U.S. What do you think is next for the gaming industry in India? Are we carving a niche?

Metaverse is a term that's thrown around very loosely, similar to how people write 'Sapiosexual' on their Bumble bios, but no one understands it. One must think about where the energy and attention are being channeled now as compared to earlier. That gives you a pattern. From the outdoors to television to now mobile phones, the effort and attention is slowly diverting. Undoubtedly, wherever energy and attention go, money, resources, and engagement follow. Humans have an anti-boredom drive, a fundamental need to be engaged, which can be proven by how our ancestors lived. Those who would plan and keep moving would live longer than those who would just eat and sleep under the shade of the tree. To answer this question, the fundamental need to be engaged is something that gaming will help in.

Are you planning to move into fantasy gaming?

There is a thesis I like to believe in: There has to be a head start. For every category leader, there are fun and games, and the market also values you differently. So, if we want to do something, we'll do it very innovatively. Are there enough motivations that we'll make a game on it? 100% yes.

There was a rise in the gaming industry during the pandemic. Was there a dip post-pandemic, and did you have a strategy change to accommodate that?

One has to keep people engaged. The gaming industry saw a surge during the pandemic as people spent more time at home, but naturally, there was a dip post-pandemic as the initial excitement decreased. However, the industry has stabilized at a higher baseline than before, which is obvious after such peaks. While the engagement level has reduced, it's important to recognize that the growth rate remains steady, driven by factors like new smartphone adoption and the evolving ecosystem in different countries. Essentially, the market continues to grow, even if it's at a more sustainable pace.

Can you share a glimpse of what the vision for the next version of the company looks like, wherein Zupee is a neuroscience company?

We are in the process of figuring it out. The ultimate goal, which is a bit aspirational too, is: Can you design a product for enlightenment? That is the ultimate product one can design, and that very thing is the goal. Sure, it will not happen through the first product or its many iterations. Maybe there will be multiple pieces of the puzzle that need to come together, it could be anything. But that is what I aspire to do, and it is a personal goal I keep for myself because it highly resonates with me.

Saurabh Garg

Saurabh Garg is the co-founder of NoBroker, India's first PropTech unicorn, and an alumnus of IIM Ahmedabad and IIT Bombay. He founded NoBroker in 2013 with his co-founders, Akhil Gupta and Amit Kumar Agarwal. Before this, he was with The Four Fountains Spa, the largest scientific health club, and has also been a part of the sales and marketing team at Hindustan Unilever Limited.

Being an influential angel investor, he has backed over thirty startups and plays a crucial role as an advisor and mentor to several early-stage companies. As the co-founder of NoBroker, he has transformed the real estate landscape, creating a revolutionary platform that eliminates brokerage fees, making it simpler to buy, rent, or sell a home.

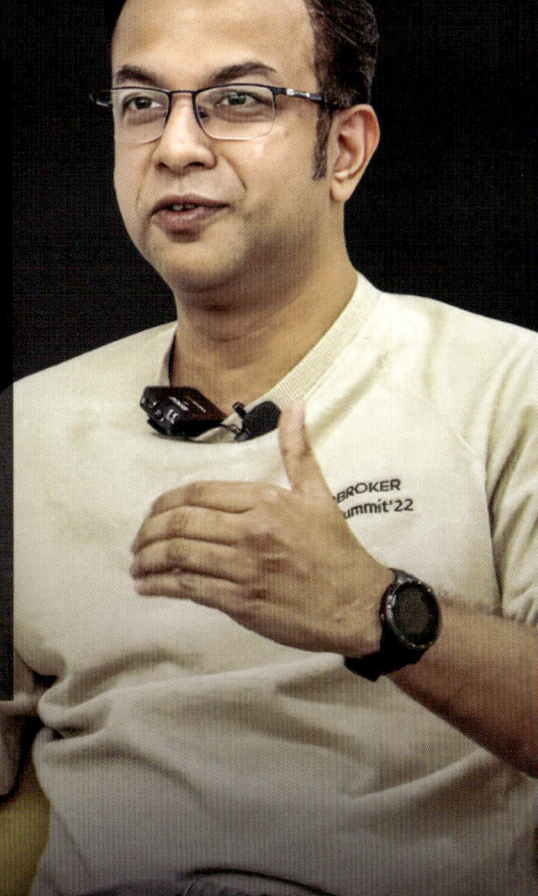

CHAPTER 11

The No Broker Approach to Real Estate in India

In conversation with Saurabh Garg, Co-founder and CBO of NoBroker

Entrepreneurship is a tricky road, but coming from a family of doctors and engineers, Saurabh Garg always had an itch to scratch entrepreneurship's surface level. After facing many complexities that come with brokerage in India, he has been on a mission to get people their dream houses with NoBroker. In this conversation, he addresses what led him to jump from working at a conglomerate to solving problems by launching his startups and his different stints at it.

He also delves deeper into the impact of the dot-com season and what opportunities real estate in India has. From discussing monetization models to the threats made against him from brokers around the city, Saurabh takes the reader on an honest journey through his many failures and challenges.

❖ ❖ ❖

The conventional path for many often involves pursuing engineering, followed by an MBA, and gaining a few years of work experience before transitioning into entrepreneurship. In your view, when is the right time to leap into entrepreneurship?

There is truly no right time. Coming from a family of conventional professionals—engineers and doctors—I always had an itch to explore entrepreneurship. Problem solving was something that really excited me, and my first attempt at entrepreneurship took place back when I was studying at IIT Bombay in the year 2000. The idea was built with one of my friends, and we had read that the franchise business is going to be huge in India; so we built a model for franchising where one can list and others can connect them.

This was right when the dot-com boom had happened, so no one was ready to fund this idea, and we shelved it right there. Then, there were other ideas that struck me, and I kept trying on my own time till my graduation from IIT.

Later, when deciding on a college for my postgraduate degree, the choice was between Columbia University in New York, Imperial College in London, and IIM Ahmedabad. I chose the third because the growing opportunities in India interested me. After this, I worked at HUL for over three years. I was twenty-three years old at that time. I was exposed to leadership, which was incredible since I had colleagues who were twice my age, and there was a lot for me to learn. Entrepreneurship is a very personal and subjective journey, so whenever one feels that the time is right, they should just dive in.

Did you witness pushback or encouragement before starting NoBroker and, more specifically, while entering entrepreneurship from your family?

Entrepreneurship is a tricky road, and my father, specifically, was a huge supporter of HUL. For him to realize that I was moving on from such a huge conglomerate to start something of my own was a hard pill to swallow. But it all came through, eventually.

It's a common saying that finding the right life partner is a nightmare, and so is finding the right co-founder. How did you navigate this process, and what factors led you to finalize your co-founders?

It's true that finding a co-founder is probably as big a decision as finding a life partner. Fortunately, when we established NoBroker in 2013, I had already known my co-founders for almost a decade. Akhil Gupta was my junior at IIT Bombay, and we were next-door neighbours in the hostel, while Amit Kumar Agarwal was my batchmate at IIM Ahmedabad.

It's critical to find the right co-founders since you will undeniably spend the better part of many days with them. There will be arguments, backlashes, and conversations. And for these to happen openly and in comfortable spaces, one needs people whom they can trust and rely on with the business they are building. That's how it was for me with my co-founders. That's the level of comfort one needs to be at to build a business the right way.

In our case, our families know each other, and our kids play together. That broadens many aspects of work for us. Sometimes, we travel together and blend different aspects of our lives so it forms a family.

What has the journey at NoBroker been like? Has that lived up to the vision you planned back in the day?

NoBroker's idea was instilled when I struggled to find a house in Mumbai. The first time I went house hunting after quitting HUL was a tiresome experience. The houses the brokers showed were in terrible shape. After many hassles, when I found one through a broker, they asked for ₹45,000 as brokerage, which was a hefty amount to pay without any earnings or no funding in place. Eventually, after I signed another lease the next year, the brokers quoted the same amount, citing that it was a common practice. I realized that a million others like me would be struggling too, so I decided to solve for that.

I booked the domain name NoBroker in 2007. At the time, I was occupied with The Four Fountains, my first startup, so I didn't focus on NoBroker as much. Later, in 2012, I spoke with my co-founder Akhil, who was in Bengaluru and had observed the same problem. Amit, our other co-founder, was also looking to switch jobs, so he joined us. It was then that we quit our respective jobs and businesses and joined in to start NoBroker.

The core idea was to help people find a home—rental, buying, and selling were the segments we envisioned launching.

A real estate journey is far more complex than it appears. Homeowners looking to sell properties or put them up on rentals face challenges related to the furnishings of the house—cleaning, repairing, and painting. Usually, a broker would get that done. In our case, NoBroker pitched in to say we would get it done, which gave birth to our 'services' vertical. On the other hand, those looking to move houses needed movers and packers, home loans, rent agreement services, and the like, so we soon catered to that as well. Everything one needs to take care of in a real estate journey, NoBroker does that. We trickled down to become a one-stop shop to solve all the pain points a homeowner, a tenant, or a homebuyer faces.

Securing the first round of funding is a pivotal moment for any startup. What made you decide that it was the right time to seek funding, and how did you identify the right investors?

We realized early on that we would require funding upfront since we were a consumer tech startup. We launched NoBroker's platform and went out to raise money, but we faced quite some inertia and pushback as there was no such model or any scope for it in the U.S. or China.

Realistically, these countries already had models and structures in place for brokers since the markets are regulated. So that was one challenge we faced, and we struggled for the better part of a year.

As we were about to close term sheets with an investor, there were media reports that Housing.com had raised about $90 million from SoftBank. Instantly, the entire environment changed, pushing us further down, as this was one of the biggest players and the largest fundraisers in this space. To build any startup, persistence is the key that keeps you going on and on despite the failures and challenges.

After that hit, we kept on executing and exploring. We realized that the number of transactions we were doing in the cities we were present in was higher than those recorded by the bigger champions in the market. Eventually, it narrowed down to convincing that one investor, and that one investor became Elevation Capital for us. They invested about $3 million in NoBroker, and that's how we pivoted.

What is one unforgettable memory from your first startup, The Four Fountains?

We were naïve, and soon after launching our first branch, we gave coupons to ShoppersStop. We hoped that if we gave them 100 coupons for further redemption at the branch, 100 customers would come in. That was all the space we had—we could only accommodate 100 people. Surprisingly, out of the 100, only one came through, so the conversion rate was very low. We should have identified that and given 10,000 coupons instead for a conversion to 100 customers.

India's real estate market is enormous, and NoBroker has been reshaping the industry for some time. What recent developments have been unfolding on your end, and what can consumers specifically look forward to?

The real estate market in India is undoubtedly huge; the numbers support that statement. As a matter of fact, consumers like you and I pay about ₹1,50,000 crore each year just as brokerage, which is shocking for India. That's not a number that contributes to buying a property; rather, it is simply something you and I give to someone who has just helped us find a place—be it an office space or a house.

So far, we have just scratched the surface. Through NoBroker, people have rented about 60,000 houses, and we sell about 5,500 houses month on month. Overall, this becomes about $9 billion worth of gross merchandise value (GMV) each year, but broadly, this is a very small part of what we do. Every year, we save around ₹4,000 to

4,500 crores in brokerage, and that is just 3% of what people spend on brokerage across the country. This is not a bad start, but there is a lot we want to do.

An article mentioned that a group of fifty to sixty traditional brokers trespassed and vandalized your office in an attempt to shut down NoBroker. How serious was the situation, and how did you handle it?

Soon after we got our funding, we had hoped to get an office space for us—nothing traditional but more of a casual, informal setup—and we found a quaint bungalow in the HSR Layout neighbourhood of Bengaluru. Before that, we'd been working from Akhil's home for about a year or so. One unfortunate day, a crowd trespassed our office, hurting some employees and destroying our belongings, and the police were called to get a hold of the situation.

We had to vacate our office the same day because it certainly was not safe to work from there. Again, for a couple of months, we didn't have a space to work from. We divided our teams to work from two makeshift offices, and it reached a stage where we didn't have enough chairs and tables. We'd sit on mattresses and get the work done.

That disruption, however painful it was, taught us two things: Resilience to fight for the vision of the company and the fact that we were doing something right. If we were insignificant to the world around us, there wouldn't have been any disruption. So, it proved to an extent that our cause was right.

> *The event when our office was vandalized by a mob taught us the resilience to fight for the vision of the company and the fact that we were doing something right.*

Did it cause any fear for you and your employees?

On the contrary, the employees were confident and excited that we were making a difference. About 90% of the employees who were present at that time are still with the company as they strongly believe in our vision.

What is your monetizing model like, since you don't charge brokerage and help consumers save about ₹4,000 to ₹5,000 crore year on year?

On our platform, sellers, buyers, and those looking for rentals are free to contact the opposite party at zero cost, but there is a limit. A tenant can contact up to nine owners; a buyer can contact up to twenty-five owners. After that, a small fee is charged, which is between ₹1,500 to ₹2,000. Moreover, if you are someone who wants to save both time and brokerage, you can pay a slightly higher fee and get connected with a phone relationship manager who helps you find a place without the need for you to have any conversations.

We also generate revenue with our services vertical—painting, cleaning, movers and packers—so multiple levers keep the model up and running.

How did the COVID lockdown impact the business, given the restrictions on movement and the decline in people relocating?

Shifting homes was the last thing on people's minds during the COVID lockdown, which affected the business. But the recovery was equally fast—the demand was high after the restrictions had eased up a bit. Throughout the COVID years, we were able to scale our additional services, like the movers and packers one. In such an unorganized category, people trusted us with hygiene and following regulations while packing and moving things. As soon as restrictions started lifting and companies started opening their offices, we saw a huge demand in home buying, especially from people who were locked up inside their rented houses and now wanted to have a permanent place and security. People started identifying the emotional value attached to homes, and the significant rise and demand in the housing market can be attributed to COVID alone.

How can young professionals determine whether entrepreneurship is the right path for them? Many are drawn to it as an escape from the traditional nine-to-five or with the ambition of building a unicorn. What factors should they consider before making the leap?

There are two angles to it: Firstly, entrepreneurship is pure hard work, despite the glamour that you see on the outside. One comes across many moments where they reconsider their choice of starting their firm. A startup goes through many ups and downs, and they have to be ready to steer through it. Secondly, if you are bored with your job, that's not a good reason to start a company. You could transition into a different job rather than starting a venture of your own.

Starting a company of your own requires you to tap into the market and solve a problem better than anyone else in the market. Once that has been tapped into, then you should start venturing your own business. There are very few cases when one starts a company by accident, and it all goes well. Another personal factor to understand is, are you ready for a tough life for the next decade to make your business a successful one?

Are there timelines or targets set by founders on when they want to become a unicorn? What is the ideal thought process of founders to achieve unicorn status?

Setting timelines for becoming a unicorn is not the best way to reach those heights. Your motive should be to provide the best solution to the existing problem. The founder must focus their attention on bringing in customers. If I think of real estate as a consumer, I should be thinking of NoBroker. If that is not happening, then it's the founder's responsibility to elevate the company to that pedestal where company and category are thought about simultaneously. Valuation is the output; it should not be the aim.

I think I read somewhere that, due to recession woes, profitability is now expected in about two years from starting up.

When operations are running smoothly and both clients and investors are satisfied, what should a founder focus on to ensure long-term success and sustainability?

This begs for a very subjective opinion. Broadly, it varies from founder to founder and their goals, but considering that a company is self-funded, one may think of running it profitably for as many years as one can. Zerodha becomes an interesting case study in that matter—they don't need to do an IPO or any sales. They can simply keep running it. But as soon as you have investors on board, the expectation changes from just running the company to getting an exit at some point. However, in today's scenario, many companies have investors, and to exit eventually, there are two approaches to consider: Sell the company or do an IPO.

For new-age audiences and aspiring entrepreneurs, what's the best approach to building incremental knowledge? With founders deeply engaged in running their businesses, how can one effectively gather insights and stay informed?

One significant part of my learning has been understanding that founders need to keep upskilling themselves. To achieve this, it's essential to build a strong second level of leadership—a team that works closely with the founder to handle operational tasks and scale established processes. This allows the founder to define the vision for the company. At NoBroker, if you are unaware of the founders and you walk into our office and observe the twenty people who constitute the second layer of leadership, you wouldn't be able to guess who the founders are—all of them are passionate and push each other and us to reach the next stage.

Similarly, it's important to meet those who have faced challenges and can explain how to elevate from zero to one and then from one to hundred. One can also read about entrepreneurs and their journeys through the books they have written or the books written about their lives. These conversations and activities build perspective and often instill a vision that is otherwise unknown.

> *As founders, it is important to strike up a conversation with those who have faced challenges and can explain how to elevate from zero to one and then from one to hundred.*

Many companies have advisors and mentors on board—who are those people for NoBroker?

Officially, we don't have any, but time and again, I do go back to many of my HUL colleagues for marketing insights, and they often come to me when they want to understand how online businesses work. That exchange of ideas is valuable, and similarly, we have had conversations with people where we've tried to understand how to optimally use technologies. These interactions build a vast scope of knowledge and learning.

Do you envision NoBroker entering the same space as OYO or supplementing it or its vertical OYO Townhouse?

As opposed to our model and target audience, OYO caters to travellers and those looking for short stays. People coming to NoBroker are not clicking to have the accommodation needs for short stays fixed.

Quick Takes with Saurabh Garg:

1. **Describe yourself in three words:**
   Innovator, Explorer, Silent.

2. **One source of inspiration that you turn to in your low days:**
   Sam Walton for his book *Made in America*.

3. **If not in the current profession, then what else would you have been doing?**
   Instead of IIM Ahmedabad, I would have pursued quantitative trading at Columbia University and become a trader.

4. **Who's your favourite superhero?**

   Warren Buffet. For me, he's a superhero for his understanding of businesses.

5. **Are you a morning person or a night person?**

   Morning. I really like to witness the rising sun.

6. **What annoys you the most?**

   Repetitive mistakes.

7. **The weirdest food you've ever eaten:**

   A roasted cockroach in Korea.

8. **How many countries have you travelled to, and which one is the most preferable?**

   About thirty-five and the two I like the most are Bhutan and Japan.

9. **Any interesting things one can find in your wallet:**

   I think it's unconventional, but I never have cash.

10. **What does your weekend look like?**

    Spending time with my toddler son, reading, and listening to music on my collected vinyl LPs.

11. **One new technology that you would bet your money on:**

    Artificial Intelligence.

12. **If a movie were to be made on your life, what genre would it be?**

    Adventure.

13. **Who would you want to play the lead actor in that movie?**

    Leonardo DiCaprio.

14. **Favourite reading source to stay on top of the world:**

    Twitter.

15. What percentage of success do you owe to your luck?

A solid 49% on a mix of luck and timing.

16. What is the lowest point of your time at NoBroker?

After the attack that happened in Bengaluru, it was extremely difficult to move on from that.

17. Given a chance to acquire any of the PropTech companies in India, which ones would it be?

Nothing that tops my mind. We have already acquired one we wanted to: Society Connect for our NoBrokerHood vertical.

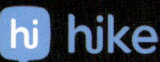

Kavin Bharti Mittal

Kavin Bharti Mittal is a business tycoon and the force behind Hike which comprises the unicorn Hike Messenger and Rush Gaming Universe. An alumnus of Imperial College, London, he is set to build solutions for the real-life problems of consumers.

Kavin launched Hike in December 2012 followed by Rush in 2021. Hike, during its older days, proved to be a force that dominated the messaging ecosystem in a country like India. He garnered over 100 million registered users exchanging over 40 billion messages per month. He has achieved many accolades, Forbes' Asia 30 Under 30, Class of 2017 being one of them.

CHAPTER 12

One Ultimate Failure to One Solid Successful Venture

In conversation with Kavin Bharti Mittal, Founder and CEO of Hike

Kavin Bharti Mittal was under the spotlight for a long time, and in this conversation, he rightly says—if it goes right, then it's sheer luck, if it goes wrong, it's because of your efforts. Founder of Hike and Rush Gaming Universe, Kavin witnessed firsthand the rise and fall of Hike Messenger, a once-promising messaging app. From its rapid growth to its challenging downturn, he shares the core problem they aimed to solve with Hike, the decisions behind pivoting the business, and the hard lessons learned along the way.

He talks about the concept of tokenization in gaming and the challenges of building networks in an increasingly competitive market. Additionally, he speaks of the potential gaming as an activity holds, and what social impact it has.

❖❖❖

Can you take us behind the scenes of your journey with Hike? How did it evolve from being one of the most popular apps to encountering significant challenges?
Hike Messenger was launched in December 2012 and in less than five years, observed an impressive rise from about 35 million monthly users to a whopping 15 million active daily users. Our initial problem

statement was: Could we use messaging and convert it into a gateway or a highway to the internet—2G data was expensive, smartphones had just entered the scenario, and it was fairly difficult and expensive to use the internet on a smartphone. That was what we aimed to solve.

Keeping that in mind, we launched Hike, SMS stickers, introduced hidden mode, and went on with that before converting Hike messenger into a super app that had other content, games, and payments. This worked great for the five years. However, it was a challenge when data and smartphones became cheap, and the market completely transformed. Our first response to 4G was excitement and curiosity as we had about half the penetration of the online market, and we could only wonder what a great wave 4G was going to bring. With cheap smartphones and 4G in the space, we were confident of growing with it, however, what we saw was shocking: Our metrics were going downhill. Users moved on because our super app—which had content, a payment gateway, and messaging—was too text and photos heavy and there was no need for one. A smartphone itself became a super app.

When we didn't see users staying back, despite the many modifications we made and the risks we took, we decided to shut shop. In hindsight, that decision was difficult but the easiest one we took at that moment. It was because we were not ready to fight a global battle with the bigger conglomerates. In essence, messaging and social is a network game, not a product game. No matter how much innovation you have on the product, if the network is not there, it doesn't move a needle. We had other segments as well—SOOPER, a share-chat content platform; followed by Vibe, an app intended to make friends that transitioned into dating, which didn't work well. The realization had hit that we had lost the battle.

> *In essence, messaging and social is a network game, not a product game. No matter how much innovation you have on the product, if the network's not there, it doesn't move a needle.*

After shutting our Bengaluru office, our focus was to start with a clean slate—so we launched our third product, a gaming one. The gaming industry was huge: In a couple of years, the market was about $200 to $300 million, and smartphones proved to be fantastic. The biggest problem, however, was that this is a low-income population. 90% to 95% of India earns less than $300 a month. So we thought, could we take gaming, which is super fun, and convert that into a new source of economic opportunity for the masses? That was the inception of Rush.

When we launched it, we found product-market fit and scaled it quite fast because we were very clear about the problem statement, and we benefited tremendously from the fact that we had learned how to build networks. It's a player-versus-player network, where the model is free to play, win to earn, and pay to participate in bigger tournaments. We have about 6 million players on the platform and of those about 2.5 million people pay because they're confident in their skills. We have fifteen games on the platform, and Rush today is now doing over half a billion dollars of gross revenue a year.

We were fortunate to find a vision that can resonate with the market, and there are only certain platforms and applications, where people play games and earn their livelihood. There is certainly a potential where people can supplement their income with Rush.

Such apps and businesses have crashed because when you have a token involved in a game economy, it's a very different beast. You're like a mini nation online and if you're printing your tokens to infinity, you'll have hyperinflation. Gaming may not just be a source of economic opportunity, but customers can become owners in the platforms they help create.

How does the token system work in the game economy? What's the economics of it?

It's all about the value. Take Facebook for example, it's built on humans and their data. We're effectively the core value. Imagine, when they're making billions of dollars of revenue off my personal data, where is my cut? It's because users don't own their data. It's all owned by Facebook. If you change that and allow customers to own their data, then all the value ascribed to things you own will come to you, as a user. The blockchain is effectively a toolkit, and a new kind of database that lets you own things in the virtual world, and thus can make them non-fungible of sorts. Can you launch a token in a fungible or non-fungible way? One that allows you to own a part of the platform? This would let you participate in the economic upside as the platform grows in value.

Now extend this in a much, much bigger way. Let's say Rush launched a token, and let's say the company is worth $1 billion. If the users own 10% of that, there's $100 million of value created for the people. Now let's scale that to the Indian economy. Let's say the Indian economy reaches $5 trillion in a couple of years, and $1 trillion came from the internet economy. We can also assume that the government was super bold and said all internet companies must allocate 10% of their token supply to all their customers. Your Indian consumers will own 10% of the value created in the internet space. It's $100 billion that could change everything including the market.

Is a gaming company, by virtue of all its externality, really net positive in the world?

The real question should be: Can we convert it to a net positive? Because there's nothing wrong with entertainment. As human beings, we need some play from time to time. The question is, can you convert that play into something more? That's our goal, and we've got a long road ahead to figure out exactly what this looks like. And I guarantee you that what Rush looks like today will be different from what Rush will look like three to four years from now.

What are your thoughts on customers potentially becoming addicted to games and its social impact?

It's actually the one thing that keeps me up at night. As a result of which we have options like smart play in our application, where if you have a small losing streak, we push you back and advise you to take a break. It's not only in the user's best interest but also ours. If they lose, their relationship with the app goes down, thus it helps if we suggest they take a break and come back later to play.

Additionally, our model currently is not such that one has to lose for the other to win. Out of the 6 million players, only 2.5 million deposit cash and play. For the rest, it's a source of entertainment.

Imagine the Rush Gaming Universe as a virtual nation that requires a passport or a visa to enter its waters, then based on access you have a citizenship or a tourist permit. Free players are like tourists who get limited access, while the ones who pay are citizens and the entire platform is open to them. Both citizens and tourists interact and trade to form the GDP (Gross Domestic Product) of this virtual economy, which stands at half a billion dollars in gross value. Like a real nation, we tax this economy—not to profit, but to reinvest in infrastructure, customer education, and overall growth.

Moreover, the way a nation has a currency, has scarce assets, similarly, these virtual nations will have the token acting as currency, and the NFT (Non-fungible Token) is going to be launched, which will become a scarce asset. Think of an economy within the walls of a country: Someone creates a good or service, sells it, and earns money in return. But in a digital ecosystem like the Rush Gaming Universe, goods and services don't rely on natural resources—they're created entirely online. The only way one player earns is when the other spends, thus making these economies net-zero by nature. So, how do they grow? The answer lies in Foreign Direct Investment (FDI). In our model, FDI could mean bringing external money into the platform: By supporting a player and sponsoring them to fuel the Rush economy.

The potential for virtual economies to attract FDI is massive.

Which state plays the most games?

Uttar Pradesh, followed by Bihar. We are very popular in the middle Northern belt of India.

What are some other interesting metrics that have come out about India in general, from your experience after working on Hike and Rush?

Only 25% of our user base is tier-1 cities; the rest is tier-2 and below. Language was a barrier in our case, so we ported the entire language medium to Hindi but other factors are that people don't read and some don't know how to read. Hence, from a UX (User Experience) perspective, one needs to build a system that has less text and more voices. Even if it needs to be through AI models to simplify the user experience.

> *Success only comes after dealing well with failure. It's paradoxical. Since our culture is very experimental—one must make bets but without betting a company.*

What's the age group of your users, as a part of the metric?

It ranges from about the first year of college goers, starting from about seventeen to twenty-eight. Then comes the group of older people who have a small business or have time on hand.

Which are your most popular games out of the fifteen you have?

Carom, snakes and ladders, then there is our version of Ludo which we call Speed Ludo—all games of ours are less than five minutes because of the bite-sized attention span of people nowadays. We also have a version called Tez Ludo, which is two and a half minutes and that's becoming a sensation.

You had a lot of eyeballs on you from a young age, and that had its implications. What was it like for you?

One's relationship with failure changes over time and with experiences. It happens because of the credibility loss that one faces in a market like India, it's difficult to stay put. Especially for someone like me, who has been under the spotlight, the model was—if you do well, people say it's tremendous luck, if you don't do well, then it's only because of you. I was quite aware of the fact that what I am running after, and what everyone is running after, is freedom—the ability to do anything you want. Hence, if Hike didn't work out, I would have to set my targets for ultimate freedom back by a long way.

Interestingly enough, success only comes after dealing well with failure. It's paradoxical. Since our culture is very experimental—one must make bets but without betting a company: That gives you leverage to try and make your idea work for the second and the third time. If someone is thoughtful about the experiment they did and failed, it's a good thing, we'll pat them on the back.

Does it become difficult for you when media representatives compare you with your father and the family?

I was naïve and foolish when I was younger, so the spotlight didn't bother me. Later, I became obsessed with building something. I was so focused on the process that I didn't notice the spotlight. It wasn't until we had to pivot the company that I became aware of it and that's when the media came after me.

We also had so much success for the first four and a half years that things were just flowing right and we were busy building. That struck a realization that society is set up to judge failure. People worry before starting something because they fear the judgement of society and the outcomes of failure.

The toolkit or the framework that I follow to overcome it is understanding the concept of possibilities and probabilities; instead of certainties. There are no certainties in the world—that a thing will certainly happen. There are possibilities—either you get hit by a car or not; and then comes the probabilities of those possibilities happening—the probability of us getting hit by a car while we are inside a house is low. But, eventually, it's all about possibilities and probabilities and that makes you comfortable with the ambiguity of how things are shaping up.

Coming from a strong family business network, do you ever feel tempted to build on that legacy or leverage those connections? With an established distribution system already in place, why not capitalize on that advantage?

At its core, Airtel is not a family business—it's a professionally run institute that serves the country and the world at large.

There was never the expectation for me and my siblings to take over the family business. As a result of that, we were raised to be independent. That gave me the space to figure out myself, and my own story. Secondly, regarding distribution, these are independent companies with their network of distribution.

How do you attract the first 5,000–10,000 users to the platform?

Weirdly enough, it starts with building a fantastic product, and then finding that one customer who absolutely loves your product. Paul Graham from Y Combinator once mentioned, 'Do things that don't scale'. It's such a fair saying—you just need a handful of customers to begin with. Show the product to your target audience and ensure it solves a real problem. If you do that, you'll get your 100–1,000 customers in the beginning.

> *You just need a handful of customers to begin with. Show the product to your target audience and ensure it solves a real problem. If you do that, you'll get your 100–1,000 customers.*

In the beginning, one's product is not at its finest—it's like an MVP (Minimum Viable Product). How do you still get that stickiness?

The MVP doesn't need to be bad, in fact, it acts as a dart game. Makers tend to ship too much in the first version. They decide that one thing isn't going to work so they put four—now you have four things to test instead of one. Ideally, one should simplify the first version, and throw that to the public. Gauge the response, the possibilities, and the probabilities as you move forward.

What kind of personal framework do you use for decision-making and investing?

Being a CEO of a company, one's mind has to move like a radar across dimensions. First, you need to understand the vision; what it is, and how that encapsulates the purpose of your company, your five-year plan, and your dream or the craziest thing you want to do. To articulate that is very important because that binds the team together. It's always better if the teams are working on something beyond themselves, or something bigger than all of us.

Second, have a set of principles. We have something called the Hike code, our value system that comprises nine codes. One of them, for example, is to be curious and keep learning. We give feedback based on the performance and the articulation of that value system. Third, find people who fit in with these principles; otherwise, you will fight internally.

Once you have these three in place, then the fourth is to go out and build the product—that includes strategy, distribution, unit economics, etc. After the product, you need a process to streamline all of the above; and after product, there is capital to amplify the said concepts. Last, but never least, comes communication that binds all of these. This is how I run the company and my mind is always circling these things.

How do you motivate employees in a remote work culture setup?

Remote work is a fairly new concept to almost everybody which comes with no playbook of its own. I was a firm no-remote-setup believer but COVID changed that. Now, if I look back, there is no better setup than this. We are a remote-first, but not a remote-only company. We meet every three months and have systems and rituals that ensure people do come together on a daily or weekly basis to have conversations.

One example is, we have WBRs (Weekly Business Reviews) and in those meetings, there could be five people interacting but about forty observers who can watch the meeting happen. The meeting comes with a document, not PPTs and for the first fifteen minutes, people observe the document and add their comments followed by discussions around those. If time permits, we open the round for the audience, who were passively part of this meeting and they can ask their questions. It keeps the whole setup very united. We have town halls wherein we discuss metrics, failures, and achievements, and then come our bi-weekly Q&As where people can ask questions anonymously.

Your target audience are those between the age range of seventeen to twenty-eight—students and young professionals at pivotal stages of their careers. Gaming has many negative stereotypes, especially in India, where it is assumed to be done by those who are idle or not focused enough. How do you address this perception?

It's important to care. But, just like movies, gaming is a form of entertainment—an interactive form—which can take more time than a movie, which is for a set number of minutes and hours. It's the fun in an otherwise boring life we lead. A while ago, an influencer's business was perceived as nothing, but now about half a million people follow a particular influencer, brands sponsor them, and the stereotype is changing for good.

Gaming might observe a similar shift in a few years now, as we are still in the early stages of that.

There are a lot of aging people who could benefit from gaming, like those with memory retention problems. What are your thoughts on working for the elderly segment?

There are many companies building puzzles and games for memory and skill-learning formats and they are quite meaningful businesses but we are not looking to pivot into that as of now.

What is your favourite question while interviewing candidates?

I do enjoy putting people on the spot since candidates often claim to have done what they have not. Apart from understanding their circumstances and childhood and how they have solved real-life troubles, I do love to ask, 'How many extra-terrestrial civilizations exist in our universe that can communicate with us on Earth?' That gives me a fairly good idea of how they made a certain assumption and their process of thinking through questions.

Would you say that one of the key takeaways from your experience with Hike has been the importance of pivoting to a focused approach and prioritizing cash flow positivity sooner rather than later?

While building Hike, we witnessed the market graph go through a turbulence of highs and lows. When we raised capital in the beginning, it was far easier than when we tried raising it the next time—owing to the cranked-up interest rates. But because we were growing and investing, we kept moving forward, but after a point, we decided to pivot the company. The fear of running out of money is the biggest lesson of all. If we didn't figure it out right and find a product that had a business model, nobody was going to fund our company, since pivots are rare in India. The only option left was to hustle.

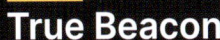

Richard Pattle

Richard Pattle is a British-origin entrepreneur who has been a pilot, followed by being the Master of the Household for the Royal Family.

In addition to his role as Senior Advisor at Zerodha, Richard served as Vice Chairman of Standard Chartered Bank. Before his corporate roles, he served as Master of the Household to Their Royal Highnesses the Prince of Wales and the Duchess of Cornwall.

With a rich background in military service, Richard spent his first eighteen years as a battlefield helicopter pilot, during which he served alongside the Indian Armed Forces in Tamil Nadu for a year.

CHAPTER 13

Lessons from Military and Entrepreneurship

In conversation with Richard Pattle, Pilot and Co-Founder of True Beacon

Through this fascinating conversation, we dive into the life of Richard Pattle, who has seamlessly blended military discipline, royal duty, and corporate success. Starting with his unorthodox journey to India three decades ago, he shares stories of his time as a combat helicopter pilot, his unexpected pivot into wealth management, and how these diverse experiences have shaped his entrepreneurial approach.

As he now leads True Beacon, an emerging wealth and asset management firm in Bengaluru, his journey comes full circle. He shares a nuanced perspective on what it takes to succeed in today's rapidly evolving business world while also exploring themes like the importance of effective communication, the growing influence of AI, and the future of young talent in the global economy.

❖❖❖

How long have you been in this country, and what brought you here?

My association with India started almost exactly thirty years ago—I had been visiting the country as a tourist, later served as a part of the Indian military, and now I call myself a proud Indian entrepreneur. I'm a firm believer of the saying that you never quite know where life is taking you, but opportunities pass all of us each day, and whether we choose to seize those opportunities is the real question.

> *You never quite know where life is taking you, but opportunities pass all of us each day, and whether we choose to seize those opportunities is the real question.*

I grew up in a wealthy household in the U.K., sought education from private schools, and lived in mansions. It was when I was about fifteen or sixteen that my parents were declared bankrupt, and we had to take all that we could and leave the house in one hour. I took my essentials, just like any teenager would: Record collections, a few school textbooks, and a handful of clothes. That's about it—I never went back to the house and never saw any of my other family members. I was born with a silver spoon but certainly didn't have one growing up as a teenager. During those days, life was looking quite depressing.

I had always wanted to be a pilot and had applied to the Royal Air Force and British Airways, wherein I failed every single application. The second time around, I had my lucky break and ended up going back to the Royal Air Force a second time for assessment. They let me in and sponsored me through university; soon, I was commissioned into the Royal Air Force.

During the jet training in those days, there was a program called Advanced Leadership Training, which allowed you to visit a country of your preference and pursue a philanthropic or leadership venture. I had read extensively about India while growing up and their age-old history. So, along with six other Air Force pilots, exactly thirty years ago, I boarded a train, went to the British High Commission, then got on a plane that went to Bhopal. I specialized as a combat helicopter pilot and did about eighteen years of military service here and served in the liberation of Kosovo in the late '90s and the invasion of Iraq in 2003.

Apart from that, I worked for the British Royal Family for around ten years as Chief Operating Officer under the title The Master of the

Household. During those days, the royal households around the world had a team of courtiers who'd help them with policy writing, speeches, etc, and in that sphere, I ran operations for the then Prince of Wales. Interestingly, there's a big focus on the Commonwealth, so they'd hire from India and across the other Commonwealth countries.

Are the lessons learnt during your time with the Air Force, then with the King and the Queen, transferable to the corporate sector?

Absolutely! The building blocks such as trust, pushing yourself, exposure to danger, maintaining discipline, and being reliant on others are incredibly transferable to the corporate sector. While you're serving in the military, you don't think that; you only find that out later.

What was your experience like as a pilot?

As a helicopter pilot, one tends to do quite some demanding flying, more specifically night flying, while wearing night vision goggles. One does a lot of formation flying, which is flying close to another helicopter going at 160 miles an hour, perhaps 100 feet off the ground at night. So imagine—night vision goggles, no lights around, and you've got a formation of four of you, and you're in a conflict.

Would you like to share some stories from those times?

There are some experiences in life where fear, urgency, and death feel very close. Being a pilot, I experienced this feeling quite often. Two incidents instilled such a feeling in the military ethos, specifically. The first was Iraq's invasion, which was a joint operation led by the Americans with countries like the U.K. And in those first few hours, there was a Sea Knight U.S. Marine Corps helicopter carrying twelve Royal Marines (British naval personnel), along with an American Crew, and within hours of that operation, the aircraft crashed with all lives lost. The entire squadron could see a huge fireball on the main route into war, and a very vivid picture of that is still in their minds. At that very moment, you would carry on with the mission because to stop the mission is more dangerous than continuing it.

> *In the military ethos, one learns to work around risk management, which is equally important a quality to have in finance and the startups that we work on.*

Another one was while we were in the skies at midnight over Oman. We were exhausted and were doing a routine training exercise while wearing night vision goggles. I was navigating while my co-pilot was handling the helicopter. He got disoriented while I was shuffling a few operations. We were 100 feet in the sky, and suddenly, a sixth sense kicked in, an instinct that something was off. I quickly shifted controls from his hands to mine and pulled the helicopter just in time. We were so close to crashing into the ground that the sand had swept inside the cockpit. A fraction of a second later, and we wouldn't be here. As a matter of chance, just two days later, my wife called to say that we were expecting our first child, and the first thought that struck me was what would have happened if she had called and there was no one to answer. In the military ethos, one learns to work around risk management, which is an equally important quality to have in finance and the startups that we work on.

If you were to design an education system, would you make a six-month or year-long military service mandatory for citizens?

I'm not sure whether it would be military service. There is something to be said for a type of voluntary service that gives young people access to different disciplines. One of the greatest gifts that I was fortunate to instill in me that came from the military was the ability to mix with all kinds of people across backgrounds. In the military, there are people from all walks of life—they could be the future kings and queens of a country or sons and daughters of those in prisons. As a military officer, you blend with everyone, as opposed to being in corporate life, where you don't get to know your peers. Hence, whether it's national service or military service, whatever gives you access and a broader perspective becomes very valuable.

How did you shift from being in the military to serving the Royal Family, to later being a Vice Chairman of Standard Chartered?

It all happened as a matter of chance; serendipity, as I call it. After being at the Royal Household, I was looking for a shift in the private sector. I joined Standard Chartered in 2014 with no knowledge of finance. Finance was not my forte, and I had one Business degree from the U.K. Back then, the former CEO of Standard Chartered advised me to join the banking sector and know all there is to know about the sector—retail, corporate, investment—and figure out my way up, back when I was forty-four.

I had already crossed my prime and was about ten to twenty years older than those working at the same bank. I took that positively and leveraged what I could do. That included putting people together, and since private banking is very territorial, I tried to stitch together an amazing community of the biggest business houses across Asia, Africa, the Middle East, and Europe.

Apart from that, philanthropy has always been close to my heart. I'm very passionate about the upcoming generations and helping young people navigate their way through life.

What convinced you to make the move to India from Standard Chartered?

It was Nikhil Kamath, whom I had met at a bar about five years ago, back when he was a successful trader and wanted to make a similar model for third parties. Together, we began True Beacon, which is a wealth and asset management company down in Bengaluru, and that's how I have been around.

Additionally, I always had an itch that I needed to scratch—India. I loved the country. When I came here as a part of an exchange with the Indian Military, I was cocooned as a foreign officer. I wanted to be here as an Indian and have a chapter of my own. The other itch was that I was handling these billionaires and talking to billionaires, but I wasn't an entrepreneur. The struggles that came with it were unknown to me, and I liked Nikhil's honesty and vision. I was almost fifty and knew that if I didn't jump in at that point, then it was not going to happen. I simply shifted gears in my life, quit the job, and moved here.

Was it a fruitful move?

Absolutely, it was amazing. When establishing a startup that started from nothing, one has to pull all strings and do all jobs under the sun on a regular working day. From meeting investors worth billions to ensuring the air conditioning in the offices is fixed. Some jobs are truly not as glamorous as they sound. In the initial days, I was absolutely clueless about many regulations and onboarding Indian clients, among many. But one has to start somewhere and build processes, client bases, and the like.

What is it like to work with Nitin and Nikhil Kamath, more so with Nikhil?

His honesty, integrity, and trust are what make him exceptional out of the rest. The fact that he was invited over to the White House by the Prime Minister to represent this country and its commerce is something we are all thrilled about. The fact that people like him who are disrupting industries are also able to participate in wealth generation is very valuable. Apart from that, he is a visionary, a true decision-maker, and great at delegation altogether.

Is his approach hands-off, or is he involved in the nitty-gritty of what you do?

He lets me be, but we are all mutually mindful of our time. He is very much involved strategically, and truly there is no one better in India to get views from on the market, the vision of the company, and the way forward.

There are visionaries who dream of ideas; then there are builders who bring those ideas to execution. What category do you think you fall under?

I'm certainly not a visionary, one who can sit and predict where the future is and how Indian and global investors are going to allocate capital to investment opportunities. I can see trends the same way everyone does, but the skills I have revolve around operations and building relationships. Building companies from scratch—even within industries you have never touched before—is incredible. It depicts something I've learned on my journey: The highest-performing teams, including global special forces, thrive on a diversity of skills, not on overlaps of professional competence. Their strengths don't overlap, but they share trust, discipline, and a unified vision, but the skillset is different. That blend is where real value lies.

One thing that has changed significantly over the thirty-five years I've been in the work ecosystem is that the average age, even in a company like ours is about twenty-eight. Coding is not my forte, nor is the manipulation of data using sample sets, but working across functions and across disciplines is indeed the way to go.

What are the challenges you faced or differences you spotted while working in the U.K. versus working in India?

Back in 2006 when I lived here, I heard a mantra that said 'India's time is now' but it was difficult to believe that, since the ingredients were not in the right place. Now, having witnessed the country over the last five years, it's clear that India is the place to be if one wants to venture a business model and become an entrepreneur. The country has got a confluence of many different things coming together—human capital, the administration has provided continuity of government here, which has propelled India on the global stage. Beyond that, this country has got a population which makes it the largest, populist country on the planet. India has a huge role to play on the global stage, and the biggest threats to humanity are centered around Sustainable Development Goals (SDGs). India, in those regards, has got a massive contribution to make to achieve those.

What do you think is the way to retain Indians in the country, especially with many leaving this country and settling abroad?

To have avenues for learners from across the world in India where they can pursue various academics is one way. To have a young college fellow from China and understand how their countries' entrepreneurs view the future of China will help a great deal. To accelerate that kind of attention and pulling power is critical for India. It's true that young fellows who move abroad for college wouldn't have a strong cultural affinity with this country. At the same time, seeing people from all across the globe in your own country changes perceptions.

What we aspire for our children is to be global, tolerant, well-educated individuals who can walk into a business meeting or a social situation virtually anywhere on the planet and not have a jarring difference of opinions. However, it's equally essential to have a very good understanding of where we all come from on this planet. Travel more, and that will become second nature.

> " *What we aspire for our children is to be global, tolerant, well-educated individuals who can walk into a business meeting, or a social situation virtually anywhere in the planet, and not to have a jarring difference of opinions, but to have a very good understanding of where we all come from on this planet.* "

What are the opportunities like in the wealth management industry? How does it operate, and is it something one must venture into as they graduate?

There are many avenues in wealth management, and one needs to zero down on what avenue they want to pick for themselves. Zerodha becomes a great case study of how in an industry, you can have the status quo for decades and then suddenly change it. Eventually, technology is going to play an even larger part, and one needs to tap into where tech and, in particular AI are going and understand which industries are going to be most disrupted. Before that, find something that you absolutely enjoy doing and then switch gears to try out other avenues. More specifically, consultancy might be absolutely high on the list for AI, but it's important to match your career with skillsets and your idea of enjoyment to a decent degree.

Secondly, before starting one's venture, one must try and do a year or two in the mainstream companies, tuning the poacher-turned-gamekeeper approach, so they can understand what the status quo is and how you could disrupt one thing or the other. Finally, wealth management depends on what type of client you have because they are dominated by relationships and are less open to disruption by technology.

We need to be more agile about investors. I think five years ago, an investor was given the entire reports of the way you are going to monitor their investments, etc. by their financial institution. It was a one-size-fits-all approach. One client of a particular age group might never want to talk to a relationship manager, counterintuitively, and just want a tech solution, whereas the other wants a good, old-fashioned relationship manager to play an active role.

It is a common saying that AI is a much better fund manager than human fund managers. With time, it's an assumption that it will only improve, and then a lot of wealth management and private banking would be about bringing in more clients and increasing

assets under management. What's your division like at True Beacon with the thirty-odd people that you have on your team?

We run two verticals within the company—one is to manufacture products, which essentially includes being a fund manager for both alternative investment funds, pooled investment vehicles, and portfolio management services. That's the model for portfolio building for our clients. The other is wealth management for a handful of clients, and that is across all asset classes. What we need is an incredible pool of young people who are derivative traders, equity analysts, researchers, and brokers. Apart from that, we need tech to analyze ten years' worth of tested data across the whole NIFTY universe. We need to buy that data publicly, synthesize that together, and then we need those who are fantastic at coding and marketing and communication specialists because we don't do any partnerships and, of course, relationship managers—it's a whole wide spectrum in itself. Before diving into finance, I had a preconceived notion that finance would be the most boring job on the planet. But when you widen your reach, the clients you have represent every single industry on the planet. Being in a client-facing role is the broadest job one can have.

Why should young graduates consider True Beacon as a potential workplace?

A small and young company like ours is very different from a well-established multinational Indian finance house. Your ability to learn and be given responsibility, by definition, is going to be larger in a smaller organization. And so, if you turn up on day one and you have a hunger to learn and propose ideas and changes, we'd be happy to inculcate them faster and launch pilot modes faster than the bigger organizations where processes are already set in place. Wherever you end up next, you probably need to do a bit of brand building and have the ability to seize an opportunity and deliver on it. It's possible not to do things the way they've been done for decades but to do things in new ways.

Sales is an avenue that is not considered at par with finance or consulting. Young graduates today want to deviate from that and stick to the latter two. How does one try to keep sales, a segment central to any organization, an area of interest?

I prefer to use the term effective communication, instead of sales. For all of us, no matter what we're doing in the world, communication is absolutely front and center of what we need to do. If you don't communicate, you wouldn't be here. Despite the great universities you have got on your CV, if you don't know how to sell yourself considering the competition, then it's incredibly difficult to get through. As founders, CEOs, and representatives of companies, one needs to know how to sell, and similarly, it goes for an applicant for a job role. Every single day you turn up, you have to sell yourself to clients and your boss. Does that mean that we all need to be on the top right corner on the spectrum of being an extrovert? No. But I had to communicate and build that skill for my job. I had to start standing up in front of people giving speeches, and without the ability to project your brand, you are left dependent on others to represent you. That's not disastrous, but if you're going to be a startup founder and you don't enjoy communicating, then make sure that your co-founder is there to cover that segment of the brand for you.

What's the vision for True Beacon going forward? What motivates Nikhil and you?

He'd been a private banking client, and I'd worked for a private bank, and together we wanted to change how we could service the needs of high net worth and ultra-high net worth individuals. We've always been focused on three things—creating great products, being very competitive with our fee model, and building a community of amazing entrepreneurs, from C-suite leaders here in India to the double-digit billionaires, and connecting those people and making it valuable for them. Not just making a blind investment that you could put in any wealth management house across the world, but bringing it alive and giving it strategic value. If you can give your business strategic value, then your clients do business with you, not just for the day job of what you do, but also the relationship and the value it adds.

Shashank Mehta

Shashank Mehta is the founder of The Whole Truth, a 100% clean-eating brand driven by his commitment to wellness, transparency, and authenticity. His journey began with personal struggles—once weighing over 100 kg, he transformed into a marathon runner, inspiring him to create a brand that prioritizes honest, sustainable nutrition.

Before launching The Whole Truth, Shashank worked at Hindustan Unilever Limited (HUL) and Faasos, gaining valuable industry experience. His leadership style is shaped by his diverse skill set and dedication to creating genuinely healthy products, disrupting the FMCG industry with a fresh, no-compromise approach to clean eating.

CHAPTER 14

The Whole Truth and Transparency

In conversation with Shashank Mehta, Founder and CEO of The Whole Truth Foods

In this conversation, Shashank takes the reader behind the scenes of his personal and professional life that led him to create **The Whole Truth**. He discusses how his early struggles with weight loss and his own experiences with food led him to create a product-based company that prioritizes authenticity and transparency over conventional existing marketing tactics.

Shashank shares crucial lessons learned from his stints at **HUL** and **Rebel Foods**, focusing on the significance of being a generalist and understanding multiple facets of business to become a well-rounded leader. Shashank sheds light on the critical role that investors play, not just in financial backing but in being key sounding boards for business growth.

❖ ❖ ❖

Let's explore your story beyond the well-known highlights—what are some lesser-known details that our readers may not be familiar with?

I come from a standard middle-class background. My father's career spanned four decades, and my mother served as a government mathematics teacher for a solid thirty-five years. I still remember that my first paycheck at HUL was the same amount as my father's last paycheck when he retired.

Back in my school days, I was a fat kid, and truth be told, many teenagers only get concerned about how their bodies look when they feel attraction towards others. Specifically, when they feel that the opposite sex is observing them. Being in an all-boys school, that was never a concern, so I stayed fat till I graduated school.

Soon, I started college to pursue engineering, and only about 10% of the class were women. That was enough for me to react with questions and statements like 'Why does no one like me? It must be because I'm fat.' I then worked hard to lose weight. However, the graph kept on dwindling with its ups and downs—I'd lose 35 kgs and in three years, would gain it all back. Then I'd lose 30 kgs and in three years gain 25 kgs back, so I did this plus minus cycle thrice in life till I was twenty-six years old.

It was only after the third cycle that I told myself that enough is enough. I needed to dig to the bottom of this and understand the science behind it. It was then that I started researching about food and fitness and started writing a blog called 'FITSHIT'. That's why the company is called FITSHIT, and that's how The Whole Truth began.

This is a familiar story for many—rapid weight loss followed by regain, often due to a lack of understanding of the fundamentals.

One only learns from their own experiences, and I, for one, used to treat it as an intervention. Ten months of constant madness of calorie counting, not eating, and running. And then comes a point when the goal is achieved, and I would feel liberated to live my life again the way other regular-sized people do. It's only when the switch flips that you realize that it never ends. It is then that one realizes the need to discover a sustainable model to make it work.

Your career began at HUL, followed by Rebel Foods, and then another stint at HUL before launching The Whole Truth. What

were some key lessons from this journey that shaped your approach to building the brand?

Most of what I do has been shaped by my learnings from either HUL or Rebel Foods. A key takeaway from both companies is their generalist approach. While HUL focuses on shifting roles across functions, Rebel Foods introduced me to the EIR (Entrepreneur In Residence) approach, a concept I only learnt at Rebel Foods. Unlike Procter & Gamble (P&G), which hires for specific roles, both HUL and Rebel Foods believe in building well-rounded leaders who can understand multiple segments of a business. Especially considering that our model was not one where you need absolute specialty, like Tesla, for instance. We focused on the generalist approach, too, since we believed that one needs to do and understand every part of the business. You don't have to understand it at the 99th percentile, but perhaps at the 80th percentile, and for the remaining 20th percentile, you need to know the right questions to ask and then hire for those specific skills.

A key lesson from HUL was leadership. Despite working under many people with unique leadership styles, the effectiveness of it was incredible. That taught me there is no one type of leadership, and you can always find your unique way. There are, however, baseline rules, principles, and questions, and one fundamental question is, 'Why should someone follow you?' The ideal answer to this is that they follow you out of respect or love, and for spectacular leaders, it's both. At Rebel Foods, the biggest learning was failure. The job absolutely burnt me out. Surely, in one's youthful energy, you can apply yourself to anything, but as you grow, it also pays to know your weaknesses. There are two ways to live: Either by doubling down on your strengths or by spending time managing your weaknesses.

> *You need to be able to do and understand every part of the business. Maybe not at the 99th percentile, but at the 80th percentile, and for the remaining 20th percentile, you need to know the right questions to ask.*

We are told our areas of improvement, but the better way to live life is to find your strengths and then create a world around you that plays to your strengths. Tendulkar has spent 10,000 hours practicing cricket. If I spend the same time, I will still not be as good as him because he has some innate strength. If you want to become world-class at something, take a strength and triple down on it, rather than continuing to worry about making your weaknesses better.

You've spoken about tripling down on your strengths while also emphasizing the importance of a generalist approach. How do these two mindsets come together in your decision-making and work?

One of my core strengths is context-switching. As a founder or CEO, your time is your employees' time. A founder is always juggling between meetings and contexts—from sales to marketing to product or supply chain. Everyone expects the founder or the CEO to know all contexts at all times, and no one tells you how to learn the art of context-switching. But it's one critical quality you can build within yourself while you are leading a multivariate functional team. Essentially, how do you hop from one meeting to the other and completely erase what happened in the last meeting.

That's a strength of mine, and that's how I marry these two. Being a generalist doesn't mean that you don't have any unique strengths. It's just a different dimension of strength. Having multiple strengths means your core strength is how you move from one thing to another without missing a beat.

Our students work on a dropshipping project for a few months. What key areas should they focus on to gain insights and skills that will benefit them in the long run?

Instead of focusing too much on dropshipping, which means that a similar product is sold by multiple businesses, focus on storytelling. For instance, if your target group is grandmothers, find a way to generate storytelling for that particular group, which will be very different from the storytelling aimed for a younger audience. Think of what will hit the right chords with them.

If you are selling a product that is sold elsewhere, too, one thing that makes your product stand out is your storytelling. Storytelling in one target group's language is a great skill to learn because you are selling a very similar product, but people will buy yours for your unique storytelling.

You mentioned that two months aren't enough to educate consumers. When it comes to product marketing, how do you ensure clarity? Should the focus be on addressing one specific need, or is it more effective to target a broader audience?

If I had to approach this within a short time frame, I wouldn't focus on deep education. Instead, I'd put it this way: If you can't find at least a 100 people who, when you tell them about your product and its value, immediately say, 'Shit, this is what I was waiting for', then it's not worth pursuing. There will always be 100 people who truly need your product and believe the world would be better with it—just find them. If they don't exist, then reconsider the work you're doing.

> *If you can't find at least a 100 people who, when you tell them about your product and its value, immediately say, 'Shit, this is what I was waiting for', then it's not worth pursuing.*

If you were a part of this cohort, what would your approach be if you had to raise ₹10 lakh of revenue in less than two months through dropshipping?

In all honesty, real life and the world don't operate like this. If you accelerate to raise this revenue in such a short period, more often than not, you'll make bad decisions. While this is a fun activity, this doesn't mirror how real challenges are faced and fixed. I am bad at making decisions when I am put on the spot. In those times, I ask my team what would change if I were to make my decision tomorrow. What changes is the sensibility of sleeping over it, forgetting it, and then deciding with a thoughtful mindset, and that's critical.

Circling back to the question, the way I would approach this problem statement is by considering the two fundamental constraints that exist. One is the time wherein you only have two months to do something and identify a space that has a very clear need or a gap. This gap is something that I don't have to create or explain if it exists. For instance, it takes years to get educated, and that's not something you can do in two months. The second action I would take is to think of the unique position I am in. For example, someone I know is in a business from where sourcing and procurement is easy, so that helps me save time because it's a constraint. My argument is simple: Someone who spends fifty-nine to sixty days selling an average product will likely sell more than someone who spends thirty days selling a great product. This happens because of communication asymmetry. By the rule of compounding, if you start selling on day two instead of waiting for perfection, you'll succeed. The key is to target the right cohort, even if it's a small group.

Besides financial backing, what other strengths do investors provide to your organization?

It's very subjective, depending on the founder and the investors involved. In my case, I brought industry experience to the table, a segment where I didn't need my VCs' or partners' help. Since they have been doing it for many years, they understand not to interfere in the founders' strengths. Their task lies in simply bolstering up wherever the founder has a lacuna. For me, the gap was that I had a weak network in the startup industry. So, if I needed some help with payroll solutions, insurance for my company, or having a conversation with a founder who solved customer experience quite well, then they were the people I reached out to for help, and they made it work. These are some of the biggest benefits they bring to me.

Other founders, however, might need industry expertise if they haven't worked in a similar industry before. In that case, the VC will help you get connected to the industry insiders. Lastly, as the company grows, your VC becomes a part of your board, and their job then is being a sounding board and a mirror for you. They shouldn't lie to you and yet not be overbearing. It's a difficult balance to achieve where they're supposed to tell you how they feel, the problems that might arise, and what could be going wrong but also be wise enough to know that the final decision of running the business lies with you. That's another key role that the VC, who then turns into your board, plays. You would want an institutional person there who has a depth of experience.

> *The job of the VC is to be your sounding board and mirror. They're supposed to tell you how they feel, but be wise enough to know the final decision lies with you.*

We've chosen three business models to pitch their products, distribution channels, and brand one-liners to you. What tips or strategies would you offer them to help them reach their ambitious target?

1. **Company A:** We are a one-stop solution for all your pet's needs. The idea was born when I got my first pet and ended up spending ₹5,000 in just two days. The problem was the lack of variety—there was only one major brand, and I saw an opportunity to make pet products more affordable and diverse.

   Our goal is to introduce a wider range of grooming products and toys. However, our biggest challenge is that suppliers are reluctant to support the dropshipping model which we prefer. Instead, they push for bulk orders or inventory stocking, making it harder for us to operate as we envisioned.

The option you are left with is to figure out the demand, and to reach that, you need absolute focus. Don't sell fifty products or stretch yourself too thin because the supply will not change. Find two products that you believe are core products and will be the easiest to sell. This is a common challenge faced by young businesses, especially considering that you want to sell your products at an affordable price. This can be done in two ways: Either create consolidated demand in one or two products or figure out a way to create pre-orders and create scarcity in the minds of consumers by sharing that you have limited inventory. That will help you create your first certain customers.

2. **Company B:** We moved into a hostel in Gurgaon and observed how hostel owners are unable to provide essentials and utilities such as tissue paper or clothes drying stands. We tapped into it and figured a B2B (Business-to-business) business to help hostel owners provide these to the residents, wherein we would be the suppliers. However, we are facing a challenge in piercing through D2C (Direct to customer) and whether we should go for a website or list ourselves on marketplaces, as there might be cases when a resident might want to subscribe to these models without the owner's interference.

With quick e-commerce already established this widely, I don't see the value in creating this D2C model. If anyone needs a box of tissue paper, they'd quickly order it and get it in under ten minutes. As you dig deeper into this D2C model, you'll realize that you want to build a quick e-commerce, and it will then strike you that the models already exist, thus eradicating the need for yours. For B2B, you've already figured a deal, and there's still some scope to crack it further there, but not necessarily in the D2C model.

3. **Company C:** Our focus is to sell spiritual jewelry and accessories, evil eye items, auspicious stones, and the like. Our one-liner is: 'Bless you and yours!' And one of our aspects is competition, wherein we have to make ₹10 lakh in sales. To reach that target, we are tapping into Amazon, Instagram sales, and the website model. If we just have two months to raise ₹10 lakh of revenue, where do you think we are on our strategy?

I am truly unaware of the market gap this model has. But my advice would be to stick to one channel, either Instagram, which is more discovery-heavy, or Amazon, where people go when they know what they want. Focusing on one of these two will help you understand your consumer and if the need truly exists. If you focus on too many channels, then your focus is going to be diluted, which is not good for the aim that you have set for just two months. This also seems like an impulse purchase, so Instagram is a great place to do that.

Tarun Sharma

Tarun Sharma is an electrical engineer turned co-founder of one of India's most talked about skincare brands: mCaffeine. He is the one who turned caffeine into a skincare revolution, and his path to this success is full of unique twists. From scaling a food delivery chain startup to running a salon chain, Tarun has seen the startup world from all angles.

CHAPTER 15

Building on Coffee in Unusual Ways

In conversation with Tarun Sharma, Co-Founder and CEO of mCaffeine

In this conversation, Tarun, the face of mCaffeine, discusses his journey as a technology professional who transitioned into the skincare industry. Tarun goes on to detail the challenges, pivots, and lessons learned from launching and scaling businesses.

Along the way, Tarun discusses the importance of co-founders and the dynamic relationships that help build successful businesses. Drawing from personal experiences, he emphasizes how complementary skill sets and deep connections form the foundation for a strong partnership. Through their stories, we'll uncover the essence of entrepreneurship, the trials of innovation, and the key to selecting the right team to bring a vision to life.

❖❖❖

Having pivoted from your career in technology, what inspired you to transition into the skincare industry with a specific focus on coffee-based skincare?

Initially, I wanted to pursue commerce, but my father encouraged me to pursue math and engineering. I obliged and, on clearing IIT, went to study electrical engineering at a college famous for mining, since my rank was such. However, the college was great, and I learned a lot.

I juggled different projects during my college days, and when nearing graduation, I was unclear about the path forward. During my final year of college, I earned about ₹5–6 lakh and realized that if I were to start something of my own with righteousness, it would take off.

After all this, I ended up taking a job in the computer science field. I then joined Mphasis, the software arm of HP. But even there, I couldn't wrap my head around the tasks I had, so I started exploring crowdfunding in India, which was a tough space to navigate. Till then, we didn't realize that crowdfunding in India had its limitations. While I was still exploring this, I met someone from the startup ecosystem, an ecosystem that was not at all a hype back in 2010–11.

In those days, if you worked at a startup, it was a given that you would not get married and would be judged. I took a leap of faith and joined EatClub (now, Box8), which earlier was just a food tech company. I joined them as their first employee, and the only other people in the room were the two co-founders and a chef. We started from scratch and scaled it from one outlet to over forty outlets, from three employees to nine hundred employees. I understood firsthand how a company is built. After over three years of working with them, I wanted to scratch my entrepreneurial itch, and in 2015, after having done everything under the sun, I thought of starting something of my own.

That's when I gathered my co-founders, who were busy with their jobs. We first launched a home salon service, which didn't work because it required massive funding. We then moved to a different business idea around salon products, which taught us that if you want to make it big in life, then the route is different. We decided not to pursue that idea further because the opportunity cost was too high. Instead, we focused on developing products for salons. By aggregating salons, we saw the potential for margin expansion, especially if we served our own products.

It was then that we created our first shampoo, conditioner, and face cream after seeking a lot of help from industry experts. During this time, we were introduced to the world of cosmetology, dermatology, the science of making a product, and the art of creating a brand. Then, we pivoted from salons to becoming a full-fledged consumer product brand in 2016.

It was not just about making the right product but also ensuring that you have the right brand to display that product. If the difference between the psychology of the brand and the physiology of the product is small, then you have a better chance to penetrate the market. If the difference is high wherein you're saying something and delivering something different, there's a good chance you might require a lot of money to make it work.

The essence of this long story is that nothing pans out the way you have planned it.

Since you pivoted into multiple businesses before doubling down on one, what were the conversations with your co-founders like, and what are some tips to select the right co-founder(s)?

While it's crucial for co-founders to have complementary skills—think of it as an office necessity—the real magic lies in the deeper connection. I have a good sales acumen, while my co-founders understand how to leverage technology—that makes us a powerful combination. Historically, there is no template for finding the right co-founder. It's almost the same as finding a life partner and building a business is like raising a baby: You figure things out with time. I didn't know anything about balance sheets back then, but now it all strikes me as right. Even skill sets, for that matter, which is an academic concept, cannot be common between co-founders. No two founders can have the same skill set, and in extension of that, one should be ready to diversify their avenues.

The real question to ask yourself is whether you're prepared to spend the next ten or twenty years working alongside that person. Research even shows that co-founders spend more time together than with anyone else, so one must choose wisely. The most amount of stress in your personal life would be palatable, but here, it's about survival. It's about the jobs of your 1,200 employees and the pressures from the investor. To figure all that out when you are not sure of the way ahead is a challenge. Fundamentally, the question is whether you can fight tooth and nail while you are in a room with your co-founders, but the moment you step out, no one gets to know whose decision was agreed on. It boils down to such a solid chemistry. All my co-founders are emotional partners. Building is very hard, but one needs to have a very strong comfort in building with that one co-founder.

A few boxes to check with yourself—can you work and also fight with them? Can you still ensure that you have a common ground and a common goal and you're both excited enough to build it for the long run? If the answer is yes, then comes the standard template.

> *Building a business is like raising a baby: You figure things out with time.*

How does the conversation between the five of you take place? How does the final decision happen?

We have many arguments. It is very important to have a CEO on the board whose neck is on the line, whether you are five co-founders or three. Individually, all the stakeholders and leaders are doing their jobs, but as soon as a decision is to be made that affects either of the two segments of the business, then a CEO jumps in. This decision to have a CEO on our board was made from day one.

Innovation and novelty are key to mCaffeine's success. How do you ensure that your product development is always innovative?

Fundamentally, the framework that helps us ensure our development is always innovative, runs in four aspects—domestic research, analyzing nationwide trends, data points, etc; international research, analyzing what is happening in your focused category and understanding which brand is pathbreaking; consumer psychology research, ask potential target consumers why they bought a particular product; and institutional spaces like salons and spas play a big role if you are making a D2C (Direct to Consumer) brand in consumer-packaged goods. A lot of our products and those belonging to our category first came out of salons. Essentially, if data says that a consumer wants a particular body scrub in a particular texture, that becomes a product idea for me. As I move on with that, we then analyze the breakouts that are happening in the salons and spas around.

This gives us three layers of products—crowded, challengers, and disruptors. These three layers come from different spaces and zones, so we believe that some of our frameworks trigger disruptors more while some of our frameworks trigger the crowders and challengers more. This makes sure that there is a healthy balance of 1:2:5 between disruptors, challengers, and crowders. This balance forms the framework of our product development.

How do you analyze what a particular target consumer wants, and what does the structure of creating targeted campaigns look like?

Most of the research is data-driven. Marketers today are incredibly creative because they are more active on social media platforms and know more about posting on Instagram and generating engagement much better than us co-founders. While understanding the audience has gotten inherently subconscious, there still has to be a certain structure on which you scale your marketing campaigns. We speak to about 300 to 400 customers a month even today, till we hit the 100 crores scale.

Back in 2018–20, if you purchased something from us, the packaging of those products had a customer care number, and that number was mine. I would pick up calls at odd hours because my belief said that if a customer is facing trouble with the product, I should be able to help them, and their experience shouldn't be hampered. Consumer calls such as these proved to be great data points as they served us in improving our products for the better. Consumer focus should be a top priority, and our larger base is between eighteen to thirty-five years old, with a narrower focus and maximum output from those between twenty-two to twenty-seven years old. On our average calls with consumers, we get in touch with these age ranges for about twenty to twenty-two minutes minutes, and we ensure that we speak to them. Beyond this, we check analytics on Instagram regarding saves, shares, CTA (Call to Action), reach, etc. Effectively, if you map all the data and build some very smart analytics around it, you keep on institutionalizing the insights machine.

How do you define culture in your company? What are the tough calls you had to make, and what has your story been?

It took a while for us to articulate the culture by distilling it correctly. Many things were actioned—how we work, what kind of people we find our tuning with, etc. In a cut-throat competition where you have raised capital, you have to deliver. A good example of that is a sports team, which is performance-driven. We might stay, we might lose, but everybody is driven by the performance, and not just corporate performance. In a sports team, there are set roles, be it juniors or seniors in the game. Juniors would know how to take a shot if it's their home pitch, and in an extension of that, they can tell a senior to hit the ball the same way they would. So to learn the ability to transfer and make it more inclusive, a sports team is the best example. After setting these examples, we distilled them into five Hs—hungry to make something, be it anything under the sun; hustle, in finding solutions and answers to the problems that didn't exist five years ago; honesty about whatever you are doing, your failures and your successes. These are the first three H's we follow. If you follow these religiously, then you are on the right curve. The step you will fall at is when you believe you are bigger than the organization you are building or the consumer you are serving. So the fourth H is humility and keeping complacency at bay; and then eventually comes humour as the fifth H, which keeps the surroundings light and disarms seriousness. One fun yet shocking instance that happened with us was, at one point, our supplier added an extra zero to the order quantity, so what was supposed to be 1,00,000 was now 10,00,000. Of course, everyone freaked out, and I started getting calls. We were unsure of how to take this forward, but eventually, we made it into a joke.

The average group of your workforce is young people, definitely less than forty, is that right?

Absolutely. 70% of my leadership, leaders across NPD (New Product Development) strategy, formulation development, consumer sales, supply chain, and growth strategy were all hired as freshers. Our idea is to hire early and scale their careers up.

What did your transition from D2C to now leading multiple channels for your distribution look like?

When thinking about building a successful digital brand, it's important to first understand that D2C is merely a channel—not the entire strategy. First, figure out who your consumer is. If a consumer is buying across categories from your brand, then the next step is to analyze if you are a placeholder brand for them or if you add a meaningful purpose to their entire buying equation. If it is the former, then they will forget you; in the latter, however, they will not. The essence here is to understand the consumer and create a category. If you believe that by reaching a certain benchmark like ₹1,000 crores, your purpose is fulfilled and it will not scale further, and you shouldn't speak to the consumer as much—you are mistaken. Figure out your consumer and your category, and then comes the channels, D2C being one of them. That will generate cash for the company. The moment you try to solve it without the context of consumer and category, it's going to be a nightmare. Pick one channel, accelerate that, and create a playbook to replicate your selling techniques. In a marketplace, you will directly sell to the consumer, while in a B2B (Business-to-Business) channel, you sell to the platform, and they sell it further. The idea is to figure out your channel, build a playbook, distill your learnings, and spend enough time. Put your focus on how your economics will work across channels and after scribbling that, find commonality in terms of which product is being sold and in which cities—that can help you in leveraging your marketing actions and making it efficient.

> *The moment you're trying to solve a problem without the context of consumer and category, it's going to be a nightmare.*

Furthermore, there are four Es for making a brand. The first is efficacy. Trends will come and go, but what will not change is the need for an efficacious product. If you are clear about it and the metrics that are used to analyze the efficacy, then you can move mountains. The second is ethos. A clean label, for example, comes with transparency of what has been used in your product and that it is not exploiting anything. The moment you club efficacy and ethos, it becomes slightly difficult to build the product, but it is possible. The third is experiential. A coffee cup is designed very commonly, but through packaging and through small experience pointers like fragrance, texture, and gift boxes you offer, you can make a solid identity. If you don't focus on experience, then there is a good chance people will devalue the product. Now, combining the three—efficacy, ethos, and experience—you are building an invisible emotional currency in the consumer's head at the end of the day. So, the fourth E becomes emotional value. If you keep on working on these four quadrants of the brand, the most intersection of all four will be the stickiest product line of your brand and the least will be the least relevant in the future. It's all required to stay relevant. But at the end of the day, the consumers are changing fast, so go back to the consumer and ask as many questions as you can to understand your relevance.

Fundamentally, you're a salesperson if you're starting a business, and in that, you have to sell to your team members, co-founders, vendors, and investors. Make them excited about your venture, your idea, and put yourself on the line. When we started, we did rigorous R&D (Research & Development) which we still do ourselves, so we knew about formulations a bit, but there were concepts that we didn't know, like the dynamics of the supply chain. It is essential to build confidence in others through the right storytelling. Sell yourself, and tell them what is at stake, considering your category lines are small. The focus on R&D has been there from day one—we'd get senior experts from bigger conglomerates and tell them we'd sincerely learn, and we did. We worked with manufacturers and with advisors, and we were firm that we would not leave R&D. I head NPD, and I strongly believe that consumer distillation happens right here. Secondly, we didn't have money. The easiest path to enter through the door of a consumer is to tap on a category where there's the least competition, body scrubs, for example. Nobody is fighting in that. We focused on scaling that category, and in the first 50 crores of the sales, the contribution of body scrubs used to be upwards of 50%, which essentially means we used to acquire consumers from body scrubs. Then, without spending a lot of money on face wash, which is the most competitive category in the country, we graduate from that and tell them that you like my brand, my product, and here is the face wash. The entry through the door should always be from a product that is the least competitive in your portfolio.

As an investor, what are the main key qualities or key frameworks you look at before investing?

I haven't made large investments, but when I do, the idea is to learn. What we look at is how exceptional and driven an entrepreneur is. It takes a lot of hard work to build a business. It is not about how hard you hit; it's about how hard you get hit and still stand. You have to keep standing in the ring, despite the hit that the market is forcing on you, and if you stand tall, then you will succeed. As investors, we do look for answers like why would you keep doing this for the next twenty years, what is your understanding of the business and the consumer, etc?

There are six Ps for fundamentally figuring out whether you are on the right track in the business. The proposition is one—what are you promising the consumer, and why are you doing it? It should be sharply defined and differentiated, and you must understand what the consumer wants and whether you have a foot there. One proposition builds a promise—make a product that marries or promises the proposition. You can't make a healthy snack bar with all the sugar in it. After building a product, ensure it's priced well. A ₹50 shift can make or break your product regardless of whether a particular brand is celebrity-owned. The consumer doesn't care about that, so the price should be based on the consumers' desire, not on the celebrity's preference. Then package it right—the message should be clear and impactful. Post which comes platform—D2C etc. which is followed by promotions—which could include you going in front of the camera and creating organic content instead of hiring influencers. Analyze where your conversion lies. Ensure all these Ps are stitched right, and you will be able to differentiate and cut through the clutter. Fundamentally, spend time on your proposition and product. Times will evolve, and platforms might change but these fundamental Ps might stay as they are. Keep hammering on the differentiation factors as you evolve with the brand.

About the Author

Pratham Mittal is the founder of Masters' Union & TETR. A University of Pennsylvania and Doon School alum, Pratham is a Partner at 606 Ventures, a venture fund that invests in early-stage companies. He earlier co-founded New York-based Outgrow, the world's largest interactive content platform behind companies like Nike, Tesla, and Salesforce.

Crack the Code to Building a Winning Business

What if you had the playbook behind today's breakout brands?

Launch Codes by Masters' Union isn't your usual business talk show. It's a straight-up breakdown of how real businesses grow and win. From iconic sweet shops to cult streetwear labels, every episode dissects pricing, customer acquisition, and growth playbooks of profitable brands.

No jargon. No filler. Just raw, actionable strategies to build and scale your venture.

Starting out or scaling up, this is the edge you've been looking for.

Scan the QR code to begin decoding businesses!